D0126754

HAIR

HAIR

A
HUMAN
HISTORY

KURT STENN

PEGASUS BOOKS
NEW YORK LONDON

HAIR

Pegasus Books LLC
80 Broad Street, 5th Floor
New York, NY 10004

First Pegasus Books edition February 2016

Interior design by Maria Fernandez

Library of Congress Cataloging-in-Publication Data is available.

ISBN: 978-1-60598-955-6

10 9 8 7 6 5 4 3 2 1

Printed in the United States of America
Distributed by W. W. Norton & Company

To Judit
" 'til the rocks melt with the sun"
(after Robert Burns)

CONTENTS

HAIR

TELLING THE STORY OF HAIR

⌒

T he idea to write this book came to me in a barber's chair.

I live in a small university town, and although I have a choice of barbershops huddled in sort of a collective obeisance before the imposing school gate, I choose to frequent one located in a quiet neighborhood on the outskirts. Marked by a traditional red-and-white spiral pole, the shop sits in the adapted living room of a small, white, wooden-framed cottage. The front wall of the room has been replaced by a large window opening onto the street; on the left are four bent-wood waiting seats with an end table; in the center are two swivel barber chairs, only one of which is ever staffed. The walls are bedecked with golfing paraphernalia: a picture of a golf green with a cluster of four players about the pin, a photo of Sam Snead with white hat, suspended antique chipping irons, signed pictures, and the like.

One morning several years ago, when it was my turn, I settled in the chair as usual; the barber covered me with a white cape, followed by a tissue-paper collar.

"So, what's it today, Doc?"

"Short. Light trim. The usual, but not my brows."

Though on occasion both of us share family stories—the wife, the kids—we have spoken little over the years. For the most part, we sit and enjoy the silence between the clip of his scissors and the tick of the wooden clock on the back wall. So I was rather surprised one day when he asked, "Say, Doc, what do you do?"

"I'm a university physician."

"Yeah, I know that, but what kind? I mean, what do you do?" He held up his clipper and fixed his gaze on me.

"I do research on hair."

His eyes widened and his face broke into a smile. "Aw, come on, Doc!"

"No, I really do," I replied.

"Okay, if you say so." He shrugged, still unsure if I was teasing him or not, and went back to work.

Hair as a body part meriting serious cultural and scientific attention is—and has been throughout history—a foreign concept to many people, including my barber. For him, hair is limited to the stuff on your head, which you position properly to get the right look. There is only one way of thinking about hair and that's it.

Since then, I have noticed that many people adhere to this limited and myopic view. They are unaware of the bigger picture. They see little to no relationship between hair and fur, hair and history, hair and health, or hair and basic biology. They are unaware that hair has played a role in the Western settlement of North America, in Middle Age European trade, in modern criminology, in religion, in art, in orchestral instruments, and now in modern biological research. They are unaware that there are many people throughout history who have worked with hair in very different ways, well beyond the barber or salon worker. They are unaware of the advances in science that promise new, more effective tools for hair care: tools to put hair follicles where none now grow, tools to curl hair that is now incorrigibly straight, or tools to uncurl hair that is corkscrew rigid.

These realizations prompted me, a lifelong hair-follicle scientist, to write a book giving the whole picture of hair and the part hair has played, and continues to play, in human life. Hair evolved as an environmental barrier for our primitive ancestors. When modern humans lost body hair, they appropriated the skin and hair of neighboring mammals for cover. With time, man found wide uses for animal hair, far beyond cloth. Hair, because of its unique properties, has shaped human evolution, social communication, history, industry, economics, forensics, and art. The topic is expansive, describing not only the role of body hair in sending social messages but also the impact of hair on human history, economic growth, artistic expression, forensics, archeology, science, and industry.

The common thread and focus of this book is the hair shaft, the beautiful straight or curled filament that decorates the skin surface. I tell the story from the perspective of people who have a particular interest and investment in hair, who know and exploit different features of hair, each of whom looks at the use and significance of hair in his or her own distinctive way. For the hair-loss patient or the bearded cleric, what's most important is the message hair sends. For the fur trader and wool worker, it's hair's insulating and cloth-making properties. For the paleontologist, it's the role hair has played in protecting mammalian life. For the cell biologist, it's the ability of the hair follicle to re-form itself; for the violinist, it's the bow; for the criminologist, it's the incriminatory or exculpatory evidence; for the cosmetician and wigmaker, it's the means for building a social message; and for the artist, it's the medium for sculpture. Because each sees hair differently, in terms of function and impact, each refers to the same essential properties using different words; for example, "fur," "wool," "beard," and "hank" refer variously (depending on the speaker) to an assemblage of hair, while "whisker," "fiber," "bristle," and "shaft" refer to individual hairs. From the viewpoint of the biologist, all these words refer to the same structure, though they recognize differences in size, shape, and growth density. From the standpoint of this book, as I address the larger question of how hair has impacted the history of man, I will take the biologist's perspective and refer to all these fibers as "hair" or "hair shaft."

What's described here is only the glimpse of a much larger story, for in all fairness each group of hair workers deserves its own book of equal or greater size. While exploring the diverse world of hair, I traveled widely and met extraordinary people— wig makers, artists, luthiers, criminologists, and others—on a journey that has taken me to medical clinics, patient support groups, molecular biology laboratories, dinosaur museums, fur merchant associations, sheep farms, textile mills, and hair art exhibitions. In the telling, I have sacrificed the comprehensive for the panoramic. Accordingly, not only have I omitted many people who work with hair, but I emphasized the Western European and North American experience, knowing full well that I could have told the same story from an Asian or African perspective. I made these decisions based on my own personal knowledge and on my attempts to limit the book to a length attractive to the average reader. I have tried to simplify the science and keep those descriptions pithy and illustrative. For the more inquisitive reader, I offer an extensive glossary, chapter notes, and references.

A recurring theme throughout is that all hairs, from wherever they arise—human, sheep, beaver, platypus, or porcupine—are alike, though they vary in degree: long or short, stiff or soft, black or white, sticky or smooth. So, a hair is a hair from wherever it comes. But, to begin, we must ask: What exactly is hair and from where does it come?

PART ONE

~

SHAPING THE SHAFT

1

THE FIRST FIBERS

———

The first hairs arose in a reptilelike, mammalian ancestor.

A ll biological forms at any level—whether societal, cellular, or organismal—must separate themselves from the outside in order to survive: Each must have a wall. At the societal level, that wall shields a kingdom from its enemies. At the cellular level, the membrane, another type of wall, surrounds, defines, and contains the cell nucleus and cytoplasm. At the organismal level—be it frog, chicken, or monkey—that wall is skin. Our story must therefore start with mammalian skin, not only because hair grows out of skin, but also because hair enhances the wall-like properties of skin by buffering it from trauma, protecting it from temperature extremes, and sensing the environment before actual contact.

All organs, like the hair shaft (the hair fiber) and its follicle (the hair root that gives rise to the fiber), are made of three different cell types. The first is a bachelor cell, which tends to live alone without making long-lasting relationships with other cells. These cells wander about the body, mostly within vessels as blood cells, carrying freight or messages, but always traveling and functioning alone. Eggs and sperm are examples of such cells, and they remain single for a long time; in fact, their job—finding a partner—could not be consummated if they were dragging along one or several petulant little brother or sister cells.

The second type is a cell that manufactures cell matrix, the soupy or solid materials that surround cells. By means of the matrix, such cells provide the undergirding for all body tissues and organs; they generate collagen, elastin, bone, and cartilage. Relevant to skin, these cells give rise to a collagen-rich layer of the deep skin called dermis.

The third type of cell makes up epithelium. These cells characteristically bind tightly to one another. They are highly social beings; if separated, they become fidgety, seeking to link up to one or more neighbors. As they stick firmly to one another, they make up a good cover for any biological plane, such as the surface layer of the heart or lung or the outmost layer of the skin. At the same time, they form the core of many three-dimensional organs, such as the salivary gland, liver, and kidney. Because epithelial tissues are made essentially of cells alone, they are, in general, soft and need outer structural support, such as bone, cartilage, and collagen. Thus, when epithelial cells form a sheet, such as the epidermal covering of the skin, they need a supportive underlying layer: the dermis.

The mammalian skin surface, then, is made of a multilayered epithelium, the epidermis, which lies over a thick, leathery tissue, the dermis. Infiltrating the dermis are cells, nerves, and vessels, which nourish the skin. The hair fiber coming out of the skin arises in a hair follicle, a fingerlike down-growth of the epidermis. In humans, the first hair follicle forms in the fetus as a bud at the base of the primitive epidermis. This bud projects down into the dermis as an extension of the epidermis and is nurtured and supported by the dermis.

The completely mature hair follicle consists of epithelial cell layers except for a small collagenous nubbin within its base called the dermal papilla. The epithelial layers of the follicle look like a collapsible telescope with three sleeves. The innermost sleeve is solid and forms the hair shaft, the outmost sleeve serves as a cellular wall separating the hair follicle from the dermis, and the middle layer holds and molds the shaft on its way out. Growing off the central hair follicle is a muscle, which pulls the follicle and its shaft upward after a fright or a chill, and a sebaceous (or oil) gland, which squirts greasy liquid onto the surface of the hair shaft as it grows out.

Except for the palms, soles, and some special regions (such as the lips, anus, and glans penis), hair is present on all skin surfaces. Nevertheless, humans have been referred to as the "naked ape" because, unlike other mammals, most human skin is covered by short, thin, lightly pigmented, and soft hairs—like the hair on your forehead, barely noticeable.

So if that's what hair is, the next question is this: Why did we and other mammals acquire hair in the first place? From where did it arise and how has it helped humans become *sapiens*?

The origin of hair is based on the evolution of animal life.

Life itself appeared on earth about three and a half billion years ago, surprisingly soon after the formation of the planet, a billion years earlier. The first life-forms were unicellular—simple, single, and independent. The next evolutionary step, which took two billion years, involved the formation of soft and jellylike multicellular organisms; these could survive and flourish anywhere as long as they were floating in water. For them to leave a liquid environment and move onto land, however, they had to acquire a supporting structure of some sort: Either the cells on the outside had to harden or the cells on the inside had to provide a framework. The former became an exoskeleton, a surface armor, which is seen in house flies, crayfish, and snails; the latter became an internal framework, a skeleton with a segmented backbone, as seen in tree frogs, rattlesnakes, wombats, and humans. The earliest backbones, or vertebrae, appeared in primitive fish about five hundred million years ago. It would require another one hundred million years before the vertebrates took a deep breath and made that fateful evolutionary step out of the oceans and onto dry land.

With the appearance of the vertebrates, a dramatic change occurred in the structure of skin: The outer epithelial layer transformed from a single layer of cells to a multilayer of cells. This was a pivotal event for our topic because the hair shaft and the hair follicle consist of packed cells that could only have derived from a multilayered structure. While the lobster, an invertebrate, has other redeeming features, there is no way he or his cousins the locusts (or their distant relatives, the earthworms) could make a hair shaft because their surface epithelium is single-layered. The invertebrates are able to augment their skin surface with noncellular materials, such as mucus (in the case of slugs), shells (for periwinkle) or chitinous materials (for beetle skin), but they do not have the wherewithal to produce a tissue of piled up, tightly adherent, epithelial cells like we vertebrates do.

If we extend our family lineage back about three hundred million years, we would be hard pressed to recognize any family resemblance to the vertebrates existing at the time. However, the morphological and molecular records are clear: We mammals share an ancestor with the reptiles, an as-yet unknown creature called a "stem reptile." The relationship is driven home by the example of the duck-billed platypus, which is classified as a primitive mammal. This semi-aquatic denizen of eastern Australia lays eggs, suckles its babies with a form of milk, and grows hair. In terms of classification, the platypus is a contradiction: mammals have hair, make milk, but don't lay eggs; they birth live young. It's very revealing that some of the platypus genes are common to mammals, others to birds, and yet others to reptiles. This animal represents one very early point in the evolutionary crossroad. Its genome reflects the traits making up the first, most primitive mammals, as well as what remains from our reptilian predecessor, whose descendants sired all the great landed vertebrates: the reptiles, dinosaurs, birds, and mammals.[1]

Our skin and its appendages reflect at least to some extent what this ur-forebear bestowed on us. When animals left the primordial seas for land, their skin had to protect them from a wholly new, not always friendly environment: dry air, electromagnetic radiation (strong light), oxygen toxicity, physical trauma, and extreme temperature fluctuations. This necessitated dramatic changes in the epidermis; it acquired thickness, strength, and water barrier properties. With time, discrete regions of the epidermis projected upward and folded down upon themselves, thereby amplifying their protective properties. In fish and reptiles, these raised portions formed flat and broad-shaped scales. In birds and mammals, they formed pointed growths—filaments that extended beyond the skin surface. For birds, that filament branched and evolved into a feather; for mammals, that filament remained threadlike: a hair.

Over the years, ideas concerning the origin of hair have varied widely. One current school proposes that hair evolved from the stem reptile's scales, a notion suggested by the fact that there are small hairs sitting in the hinge region of the scaly tail-skin of most rodents. A second hypothesis suggests that the shaft arose within a gland and initially served a role directing oily secretions from the gland onto the skin surface. This idea is based on the observation that all follicles have oil glands, that the cuticle layer of the hair shaft is structured to scoop oils to the skin surface, and that the earliest animals needed oil on their skin to prevent water loss. A third theory, which is not exclusive of the first two, considers that hair arose from hairlike sensory structures seen on the skin of some living fish and amphibians. These structures serve to alert the fish of an environmental danger, such as the water pulse of an approaching predator or the presence of an adjacent sharp rock.

In fact, there's a lot of evidence that the hair follicle and its shaft play important sensory roles. Studies in mice suggest that each hair type has its own distinct sensory system so that different hairs provide different types of sensation. While all hairs are invested with nerves and thus capable of perceiving movement, there are large and uniquely sensitive hairs found on the upper lip of most mammals. These whiskers are so important to mouse sensation that they have been elevated to the status of a "sensory organ"; in fact, they have inherent erectile properties, which, when stimulated, draw the prominent shafts to attention. For a mouse probing the world at night, its whiskers serve as valuable antennae reconnoitering the terrain well before a tender nose arrives.

Hair is an important sensory device for humans as well. In a common life experience, small hairs on the outstretched arm accurately perceive a close-passing person or a zephyr riding in with the tide on a warm summer day. People are also able to detect bedbugs more efficiently on an unshaven arm than a shaved one.[2]

In recent years, we have learned that in addition to its rich supply of nerves, the hair follicle is surrounded by dermal cells, which, under the proper conditions, can act like nerves. These cells contain proteins also found in nerve cells, and when they are isolated and grown in tissue culture, they can become neural. In fact, when Dr. Robert Hoffman and his research team transplanted these cells into a paralyzed rat, the cells not only supported nerve repair but they also integrated into newly formed nerves that allowed the rat to recover function.[3]

Hair also plays a role in temperature control. A turtle on a log, with up-stretched head catching the early morning sun, reminds us that reptiles do not have an internal means of generating heat. From its cool and protected bower in a deep stream, the turtle awakes from its slumber, moseys onto a floating log, and into a beam of strong morning sun; there he basks. Like all cold-blooded animals, he depends on nature's primary radiant energy source, the sun, to get started. But the smooth-surfaced skin that allows him to readily take up heat from his surroundings during the day also causes him to lose it to his surroundings during the night. That his body temperature drops during the night is to his advantage, because during these times he doesn't need high-priced fuel (i.e., hard-earned foodstuffs) to keep warm. The trade-off for his caloric frugality, though, is his nocturnal and early morning languor.

In contrast to reptiles, the earliest mammals could hunt in the cool night and early morning because of two major advantages over their cold-blooded neighbors. The first was that they were able to generate heat by metabolic processes without direct help from the sun.[4] The second was that, over eons, their primitive skin sensory filaments had increased in density to form a skin cover that served as a highly efficient insulator: a fur coat. These two features—warm-bloodedness and insulation—enabled them to forage among the nests of their ectothermic neighbors at night and hide from them during the day.[5]

Heat flows from a warmer to a cooler body, as anyone who has ever jogged on a blistering cold day knows, warming in open sunny spots and then cooling again in the shade. In this case, solar heat transmits over space directly to us, as it does to the basking turtle. But heat can also transfer from body to body by direct contact. When you burn yourself eating a straight-out-of-the-oven pizza, for example, you are experiencing the direct spread of heat from the body of the pizza to the body of your mouth. Heat can also transfer by means of moving currents of water or air, a process referred to as convection. For instance, heat transfers by convection when air blowing from a hair dryer picks up heat from the heat filament and transfers it to your locks.

In all these examples, heat transfers from a warmer body to our body. But heat can flow in the opposite direction as well, from our warm body to the cold outside. The Coney Island Polar Bear Club stalwarts celebrate New Year's Day by warming up the frigid waters of the Atlantic Ocean. Moving heat in that direction might be fun for a short while, but after a not-too-long exposure to such cold, about ten to twenty minutes, vital functions not only slow, they stop.[6]

Active mammalian life depends on a constant body temperature of around 98.6°F, and skin plays an active role in maintaining it. While skin is not important for heating up the mammalian body, it is very important for minimizing heat loss—and this is where hair comes in. Fur efficiently blocks all forms of heat transfer. It does this, first of all, because it grows as a dense array of hairs. Beaver skin, for example, has around forty thousand shafts in an area of skin about the size of a fingertip. At this density, fur is virtually an impenetrable barrier; neither wind, water, nor insects can get through. In addition, hair itself is a poor thermal conductor—eight thousand times less conductive than copper.[7] Dense hair cover also traps air, and air is an even poorer conductor of heat than hair. As long as hair holds a layer of air over the skin and prevents it from moving (convection), no heat is lost. Heat cannot transfer through the fur barrier either from the skin surface to the outside or from the outside to the skin surface. Fur surface mirrors environmental temperatures, and skin surface, under the fur coat, mirrors body core temperature. In an effort to expand that cosseting layer of air and thus enhance the insulating properties of furred skin, hair follicle muscles pull the shafts upward when an animal becomes chilled. This action increases the thickness of the fur coat and the efficacy of the insulation in all animals—except humans, of course, because we have lost our "fur." So when humans chill, although our hairs stand up, giving us "goose flesh," this ancient reflex is really just bluffing, because our body hairs are neither big enough nor dense enough to maintain the important stationary and insulating air layer.

Befitting its reputation as the fastest land animal, the cheetah can attain speeds as high as seventy-one miles per hour, but can only hold that speed for less than a minute before its body temperature rises and forces it to stop and cool off. This is not to belittle the skills of the cheetah, but rather to point out that fur limits its endurance in the unrelenting heat of tropical Africa. Because of fur, the cheetah has only a few means of dissipating body heat: stop running, get into the shade, start panting, lick its paws, or expose its non–fur covered body parts (primarily the paws and ears) to the surrounding air. If the savannah is as hot as or hotter than the cheetah, it will be hard pressed to cool itself at all, as heat flows to the cooler body. Thus, in this climate, mammalian adaptive success is paradoxically limited by the heat-retaining properties of fur, because fur prevents body heat from dissipating through it by any heat-transfer mechanism. Such an efficient cover would have prevented the evolution of man.[8]

Scientists have calculated that on a hot and sunny day, fur-covered, upright hominids would have suffered a heat stroke after about ten to twenty minutes of a nonstop walk; they just couldn't dissipate heat from their bodies quickly enough.[9] Our human antecedents needed to move around during the day in order to hunt and survive, yet they had to keep their body temperature at 98.6°F, so they needed a better cooling-off mechanism. The problem was complicated by the fact that the human's efficient evolution was dependent on a huge brain (the largest brain-to-body-size ratio of all animals, in fact) and yet brain tissue is exquisitely sensitive to elevated body temperatures: Heat stroke occurs at 104°F and brain death at 107°F. In addition, brain tissue temperature is regulated by core body temperature and the only way any animal, including a human, can shed excess body core heat is by way of the skin. For an evolving hominid, the dense hair cover had to go.[10]

Many ideas have been put forth to explain the loss of hominid body hair. One fanciful notion suggested by Charles Darwin contended that primitive males favored hairless females because hairlessness is more sexually attractive. According to this argument, sexual selection progressively led to the hairless state in both males and females.

Today, most experts believe Darwin's explanation is too simple. The most convincing recent view is that humans lost hair in order to protect their uniquely temperature-sensitive brain. It turns out that at the same time primates were growing larger brains—about one to three million years ago—they began to lose their body hair and acquire eccrine (sweat) glands. These events appear to have been linked. The function of eccrine glands is to control body temperature by liberating sweat, a secretion that is mostly water. A person can sweat as much as several quarts per hour and will continue to sweat as long as the heat signal persists, or until the person becomes dehydrated and collapses. The value of sweat is based on the physical fact that in order for water to evaporate, or transfer from liquid to vapor, it must take up heat—a lot of heat; in fact, five times more heat energy is required for evaporation than to boil water from room temperature. The trick is to have a lot of exposed body surface and enough water to cover that surface. Animals intuitively know this cooling property of water and they seek ways of exploiting it. One way is by panting, which exposes the multiple blood vessels lining the moist mouth to evaporative heat loss. Another is by wetting themselves from nearby water sources or by licking saliva over their hairless body parts. The evaporation of water and sweat gives an animal the ability to lose heat even if the surrounding environment is hotter than its body surface. For the furred animal, however, skin surface sweat is of no help because water under fur can't evaporate. By the same token, water on fur's surface will evaporate but it will not remove heat from the skin surface below the fur. Since sweating over the body is critical to heat dissipation and brain health, a luxuriant fur coat is a hindrance.

Loss of hair had a major impact on the ability of humans to dissipate heat and thus develop and stabilize a large brain, but it may also have had an important social role. Three major characteristics differentiate humans from other primates, such as chimpanzees: hairlessness, walking on two feet, and the family as a social unit. A chimpanzee mother can efficiently forage for herself and her child because she has two free hands, since the baby is out of the way, clinging securely to the hair on its mother's back. This could not work for the hairless human. Without hair for the baby to hang from, the naked-ape mother would have to hold the baby in her arms some way or another all the time, thus greatly limiting her ability to feed. She needed a babysitter, and any family member would do. Professor Shizuyo Sutou of Shujitsu University postulates that the father would have had to play this role if he wanted his progeny to attain reproductive maturity. Father would provide food and protection to mother and child and, *quid pro quo*, mother would provide all the mating opportunities father might seek. So, by this argument, the loss of hair could also have given rise to the nuclear family unit.[11]

With time, the earliest hair follicles evolved into various follicle forms and hair types. The "first" hair follicle was sparse and tiny, its shaft thin, short, and straight. With time, the original sparse growth became so dense we named it "fur." But within the fur and over the body grew many different kinds of follicles and hair types,[12, 13] and the properties of these unique hairs play an important role in the story yet to come.

2

THE WAY THEY GROW

~

A scalp hair transplanted to the eyebrow continues to grow as it if were still on the scalp.

On September 10, 2009, British prime minister Gordon Brown issued a posthumous apology on behalf of his government to Alan Turing, a mathematician acknowledged today as the father of modern computer science. In his proclamation, Brown termed the treatment given by the British government to this patriotic scholar as "horrifying "and "utterly unfair." In March 1952, under the Labouchere Amendment of the Criminal Law, Turing had been found guilty of having had a homosexual experience. He was offered the penal alternatives of prison or estrogen injections; he chose the latter. Two years later, at the age of forty-one, he was found dead, a half-eaten, cyanide-ridden apple beside him. It was a tragic end for a great scientist in his prime—and one who could have played a major role in the advancement of our understanding of hair. In fact, just months before his arrest, Turing published a paper describing the first credible (and now widely accepted) mechanistic model explaining how biological patterning, and thus hair follicle arrangements, might occur in skin.

Biological patterning refers to what an animal or plant looks like and how its parts are organized. It is based on the fact that all mature cells and their neighbors know they have an up side, a down side, a right side, a left side, an inside, and an outside. The biological question Turing sought to answer was no small problem in his day or ours: Namely, how do complex animal and plant life-forms take shape when you start out with one very simple cell?

All higher animal life-forms begin when the fusion of a male sex cell (a sperm) and a female sex cell (an egg) gives rise to one fertilized cell primed to make a whole new being. That first cell divides many times to form a cluster of cells and, though each cell in the cluster houses the same genetic program and looks alike, each eventually assumes a unique shape and function, enabling the group of cells to produce one complete baby. Some cells form bones, some liver, some head, and some toes. Turing wanted to know how a group of uniform cells could turn into communities of vastly different cells. How do cells interact with other cells or with the substances in the environment to become a finger and not a nose, a brain and not a kidney, a scalp hair and not an eyebrow hair, a blushing princess and not a boasting swain?

One can appreciate hair patterning at various levels. First, there is the arrangement of hair with respect to other hairs in the neighborhood. At this level, each follicle (and the shaft it makes) appears to demand "breathing" room so that it is comfortably separated from its neighbor. The rows of whiskers on the snout of a tiger, dog, or rat are obvious examples; not only are they present in straight lines, but the individual whiskers are predictably and regularly spaced from one another. With proper magnification, one could see that most hairs grow in an array as regular as the streets of midtown Manhattan.

The next level of patterning is the way hair falls with respect to the head and the tail. The tips of body hair almost always point toward the tail, or at least away from the head. In this position, hairs of the coat lie flat as long as the animal faces into the wind. The head-to-tail display of hair is such an inherent part of life experience that one reflexively strokes a dog or cat from head to tail. The mother cat grooms her nursing kittens the same way; if she must clean against the grain to remove a smudge, she later flattens the ruffle with a well-placed front-to-back lick. In fact, Swiss mountaineers of the last century took advantage of the natural placement of fur by attaching seal skins to the base of their skis to travel over snowy alpine slopes. They aligned the seal skin so that the skin corresponding to the seal's head was attached to the ski tip: The downhill-pointing hairs of the pelt resisted any back slip on the walk up. For the trip down, they either kept the pelt on for a slow descent or removed it for an unimpeded schuss.

Human belly hair also grows in a characteristic head-to-tail pattern. The strong and curly hair of the lower belly and pubic region of men typically grows in the pattern of a chivalric shield with the peak of the escutcheon pointing, like the symbol of Mars, toward the navel. Pubic hair in women fills the nether regions and forms a discreet horizontal line at the pubis. Above and to the side of these coarse hairs in both sexes are fine, short, lightly pigmented hairs that are barely visible.

Finally, hair shafts are patterned differently with respect to one another: long or short, curly or straight, thick or thin, dark or light. They differ in character from site to site over the body, but, because the right and left side of mammals are mirror images, there are corresponding doppelgänger hairs on each side. For example, there are hairs on the right upper arm that correspond exactly to hairs on the left upper arm. The disparity between hair types may occur abruptly, like a field of tall grasses at the edge of a lakefront lawn. Consider the very short, barely visible shafts of the forehead just before the hedge of short, thick, pigmented eyebrow hairs.

Because of the subtle and not so subtle differences between hairs from region to region, it's logical to assume that there are functional differences. Eyelash hairs are short and rigid, curling away from the eye surface to minimize particle entry. Underarm and pubic hairs are short and curled, made to prevent chafing between skins, fend off insect assault, and transport odors. Beard hairs are coarse, bushy, and curled, made to protect against trauma, harsh icy winds, and intense light. Different shaft structures translate into different services to the skin.

But what determines how hairs are placed and shaped? Turing knew that the way any organ (including the hair follicle) forms and positions itself depends on how its cells grow and move about. But he did not know what makes cells do what they do. To address this question, Turing devised mathematical models that would predict a pattern. In the end, he found that his mathematical models required three components: receptive cells, special growth factors made by the cells, and gradients formed by the growth factors in the soup surrounding the cells.

That latter term—"gradient"—describes the gradual change in density of something when going from one place to another. One can think, for example, of the gradient around ice cream eateries. If you were to visit my hometown in the middle of summer on a hot Saturday night, you would quickly become aware of two wildly popular ice cream parlors located along the main street, both equidistant from the town square. One is west of the town square; it sells ice cream in cups with small, dainty spoons. The other is east of the town square, and it sells ice cream in cones. Crowds of people buy ice cream at each of the parlors. They start licking and slowly walk along the main street to the town square because that's where the action is. Ice cream–filled containers are in highest number near the individual parlors, but as people walk to the square, the amount of ice cream in the cones or cups decreases. In the town square, all the containers will be empty. You can tell where you are in the downtown area with respect to the two parlors and the town square by considering the density of ice cream eaters, the shape of their ice cream containers—cone or cup—and the amount of ice cream left in the individual containers. As long as people continue to buy ice cream and progressively lick while moving to the square, there will be an ice cream gradient. No GPS needed here. (The critical reader will appreciate that we have not accounted for the spoilsport who doesn't want to walk to the town square or for the glutton who eats his ice cream in one bite or for many other variables that would disrupt our illustrative gradient.[1])

Now transfer the idea of a gradient back to the developing skin. In the youngest fetus, immature skin consists of a sheet of identical-looking cells. At a given moment, individual cells in the sheet start to give off growth factors, which cause neighboring cells to take some sort of action. As the growth factor spreads away from the producing cell, it generates a gradient and, because of that gradient, there will be different neighborhoods—some with little growth factor and some with lots. Cells in neighborhoods with lots of growth factor behave one way and cells in a neighborhood with little growth factor behave a different way. So, by means of growth factor gradients and responsive cells, Turing's equation predicted patterns—just as we could see pedestrian patterns forming in relation to the ice cream parlors.[2]

Turin saw the patterns, but it took the next generation of researchers—in the mid-20th century—to discover what those important pattern-forming growth factors were. But first, scientists had to develop tools that would allow them to grow almost any kind of animal cell in a laboratory flask, to isolate and analyze proteins, to identify the genes stored in DNA and RNA, and to control the expression of genes in living animal models. Using these new tools, scientists from North America, Europe, Japan, and Australia discovered that the growth factors influencing hair follicle placement and formation are small proteins that show several characteristics.

First, the growth factors never act alone: They always act as a well-coordinated team. If these factors were athletes, they would look more like soccer players—dribbling upfield, passing, receiving, kicking—than like solitary long-distance runners. Accordingly, as players have designated positions such as fullback, center, and forward, each growth factor plays a special role: Some stimulate cells to stick to one another in order to form follicle foundations, others stimulate cells to form hair shafts, and others stimulate cells to curl or color hair shafts. No one factor brings about all these changes alone; it takes a team.

Second, the growth factors can either swim from cell to cell or else remain on their cell of origin and figuratively shake hands with a neighbor cell without leaving home. However they get there, the growth factors will attach to the receptor on the outside surface of the cell. Once the growth factor binds to the receptor, the receptor shuttles a signal from the outside cell membrane to the nucleus. The nucleus ponders a response and—*boom*—it generates the signal for the cell to act, and the cell does something, like changing shape.

The third characteristic is that growth factors come in the form of both activists and obstructionists; that is, some factors stimulate the process and others prevent it. Scientists have found that hair follicle formation is ultimately under the control of inhibitory growth factors; these obstructionist factors usually act by blocking the action of another growth factor. For an inhibitor to turn on a process is counterintuitive until you recognize that the inhibitor is inhibiting the inhibitor of the activator; in other words, once the inhibitor of the activator is neutralized, the system "blasts off." If, for example, a delivery man (an activator) is trying to transport a package to you, but a hoodlum (an inhibitor) stops him, no package will be delivered. However, if a police officer (an inhibitor to the hoodlum) is able to apprehend the hoodlum, your package will arrive. Of course, the hoodlum himself could be helped or hindered by other members of his gang or he could be blocked by members of a rival gang; likewise, the police officer could be assisted by other police or blocked by red tape. So, if multiple actors play a role in package delivery, as this fanciful example suggests, a large number of decisions would have to be made in order for you to get your package. Because there are many such go and no-go steps in hair follicle formation, the system is under tight and scrupulous control. Without the multilayers of regulatory signals, cells might form hair follicles in a higgledy-piggledy array without regard to neighboring cells or might even form hair follicles in a site where they are not needed—or, worse, grow into a cancer.

Hair follicle formation begins in all mammals within the immature epidermis. But in order to grow, a hair follicle needs help from the dermis, which provides structural support, blood supply, and important growth factors. A vigorous and voluble cross-talk starts between the epidermis and dermis early in the process. The conversation between the compartments goes something like this:

"Hey, Derm," says the epidermis. "I am now sending you positive hair follicle growth factors. At the point of highest concentration, set up the foundation for a hair follicle."

The dermal cells respond by sending back to the epithelium a missive in the form of another growth factor, saying: "Okay, Ep. I'm sending you back a growth factor telling you I'm ready. But in order to move the project along, send down another signal telling some dermal cells to gather under the spot where the new follicle should form."

"Sure thing," the epidermis responds. "Here it comes, but, Derm, you've got to start making blood vessels, because those rapidly growing hair follicles will need plenty of food."

And so this two-way *tête-à-tête* goes on and on stimulating, restraining, molding, and balancing. As long as the follicle is developing, and even after the follicle is fully formed, the epidermal and dermal cross-talk continues and must continue for the lifetime of the hair follicle.

If you were to look at the epidermis of a human fetus while hair follicles are forming, at first you'd see a pattern of spots due to epidermal thickenings: the epidermal cells at the point of new follicle formation swell with expectant pride. Rather quickly, these epidermal cells grow into a small nubbin, and the nubbin grows into a finger, which extends into the underlying dermis. In time, at its deepest portion, the finger embraces a small piece of dermis, now called the dermal papilla, and then the finger matures into a full follicle with its characteristic embedded concentric cylinders: a sebaceous gland, a muscle, and, finally, the egressing shaft.

Although all mammals form hair follicles essentially the same way, different mammals complete their first hair follicles at different times. Some mammals form their first hair coat in the womb, while others form it just after birth. Cows, horses, and dogs are born with a full coat of hair, whereas mice, rats, and opossum are born hairless. In humans, the first body hairs appear during the second trimester of pregnancy but at birth the hair—except for that on the scalp and eyebrows—may be barely noticeable. Eventually there will be about one hundred thousand hair follicles on the scalp and between three and five million over the body. Humans don't normally develop additional hair follicles over a lifetime; even worse, as men and women age, the number of follicles over the body decreases.

Anecdotal observation from pediatricians reveals that kids show different scalp hair growth patterns. Some babies are born with long hair that continues to grow, some shed their birth hair after a few months and grow new hair immediately, and still others are born bald and don't start to grow hair until they are a few months old. In many infants, the first hairs float like a gossamer over the scalp. Not heavy enough to drop onto the scalp surface, the fibers point straight up and, in the proper light, form a resplendent, fleeting, once-in-a-lifetime, newborn nimbus.

We now understand a great deal more about hair placement, patterning, and growth than Turing did, but there are still aspects we do not yet understand. For instance, once a hair follicle acquires its own identity, it is no longer dependent on any growth factor gradient surrounding it. So when a surgeon transplants a scalp follicle into the eyebrow region, the scalp follicle will continue to grow a scalplike hair shaft—long and straight. We are not entirely sure why this happens, but surgeons use this property to great advantage in treating hair loss, a topic we will return to.

Clinical studies indicate that the underlying brain appears to affect hair follicle placement in the scalp. One example, the hair whorl (commonly known as a cowlick) is a vortexlike placement of hair at the top and back of the scalp. Hairs making up the whorl can rotate clockwise, counterclockwise, or a combination of both. Clinicians find that the hair whorl direction in a cowlick, which is a hair- and skin-related feature, reflects left- or right- handedness, a brain feature. In a sampling of five hundred adult North Americans, Amar Klar of the National Cancer Institute[3] found that more than 90 percent of right-handed people had a clockwise whorl, while non-right-handed persons (either left-handed or ambidextrous) had neither clockwise nor counterclockwise associations. Underscoring the implications of hair patterns, Professor Bernd Weber and his colleagues at the University of Bonn[4] reported that subjects with a clockwise hair-whorl orientation had a strong association with left-brain language dominance while subjects with a counterclockwise hair-whorl had no such association. The associations of whorl patterns and handedness are not unique to humans. Right-lateralized horses (defined based on preference of the individual horse for galloping, jumping, or dressage movements on the right rein) display significantly more clockwise facial hair whorls.[5] Scalp whorls may also flag underlying pathology. Multiple hair whorls, for example, occur twice as often on the scalp of mentally stunted children compared to controls;[6] moreover, children with multiple or intersecting whorls show a higher probability of having underlying brain malformations.[7]

These are fascinating correlations, even if we don't yet fully understand how this brain–hair follicle patterning comes about. Embryologists have suggested that the association may reflect the fact that in the very early embryo, skin and brain cells share a common antecedent tissue that divides to produce brain and skin. In any case, the observation evokes the evolutionary concept described in chapter 1 that the hair follicle evolved from, and is related to, a sensory or neural-like structure.[8]

What we do know is that, once formed, the hair follicle starts producing a shaft and undergoes a unique growth cycle. The story of that cycle depends on a very special cell. Finding that cell required yet another generation of scientists.

3

A MYSTERIOUS CYCLE
AND A UNIQUE CELL

Cells making up the hair follicle are among the most rapidly dividing cells in the body.

I n the late 1980s, George Cotsarelis—a hard-driven, no-nonsense, and appropriately balding academic—made a discovery that would redirect the course of hair biology research for decades to come. From his course work at the University of Pennsylvania Medical School, Cotsarelis had learned that hair grows out of skin from a fingerlike collection of cells called a follicle and that a follicle must regrow in order to produce a new hair. But regrowth of any living tissue requires stem cells—cells with the dual ability to regenerate themselves as well as to give rise to specialized cells. Experts in the field recognized that new hair growth requires the participation of these cells, but they didn't know where in the follicle they rest. Confident that those very special cells would enable him and his fellow researchers to clone hair follicles and consequently provide new hair for balding people, Cotsarelis set out to find and isolate them. It would take him fifteen years.

During the 19th and early 20th centuries, medical investigators first embarked on the enormous task of describing the cellular composition and organization of all normal and diseased tissues—the genome project of their day. They used light microscopes and stains, tools simple but powerful enough to discriminate between different types of tissues, cells, and cellular components. Taking this approach, a small group of British and European researchers, including Francis W. Dry, Ludwig Auber, and William T. Astbury in England, and Felix Pinkus in Germany, chose to study the hair follicle. With so little detailed information available at that time on any organ or tissue, why in the world did these scientists decide to focus on the tiny hair follicle? Human motivation doesn't change: money. Because sheep farmers and wool merchants hoped to improve both the quantity and quality of their product, they set up research foundations: the Wool Industries Research Association in England, Deutsches Wollforschungsinstitut in Germany, and the Commonwealth Scientific and Industrial Research Organization in Australia. These institutions provided laboratory support for anatomists, pathologists, biologists, and physical chemists to conduct hair research that would make the wool industries more profitable. The discoveries made by these investigators became the bedrock of what we know about hair today.

First, these scientists established that the follicle is a layered structure. Like a Russian doll or the sleeves of a collapsible telescope, the follicle consists of three embedded cell cylinders, each tucked into one slightly larger, with the central-most cylinder making up the hair shaft itself. They also discovered that the complex nature of the hair follicle extends beyond its intricate layering. Under the microscope, the whole shape and size of follicles changed predictively and repetitively over time; in short, hair follicles grow in cycles.

Today, we recognize that growth cycles are hardwired into all forms of life, be they single-celled amoebas or multicelled mice. Even cells isolated from human skin and farmed in a laboratory show cyclic changes. After all, life-forms evolve, grow, and flourish in a milieu of cycles set by the spin and orbit of the earth and the pull of the moon. Moreover, since mammalian embryos grow in the uterus adjacent to the largest blood vessels of the body, they rock to the cadence of their mother's pulse from the moment of conception. However, while all living beings demonstrate rhythms, such as sleep-wake-sleep, very few show the dramatic changes in form and activity of the hair follicle.

Actually, people in the Stone Age were acquainted with the cyclic nature of hair development well before the sophisticated wool and hair scientists of the 19th century. The indigenous people of North America, for example, understood that in late autumn, the beaver's coat displays optimal characteristics for clothing, because at this time the animal's fur is thickest and best suited to resist the ice, snow, cutting winds, and freezing waters of the Canadian winters. They had observed not only that fur growth is denser in autumn than spring, but also that no hair growth occurs during the depth of winter or the height of summer. They knew that for the best furs, they had to collect skins from beavers trapped during the cold months.

For most furred animals, hair growth starts and stops in relation to the position of the earth in its course around the sun. This solar connection means that, throughout the year, each body hair grows and sheds at the same time as its neighbor; in other words, body hairs of furred animals grow in unison, synchronously. At any one moment, hair follicles in animals ranging from beavers to lap cats are either growing, resting, or shedding. In late spring, when you coddle your cat and find gobs of fur balls on your sweater—much more than you see other times of the year—you are experiencing that period when most of the follicles are in the shedding phase.

Human scalp hair follicles differ in this respect. They cycle, but they are, for the most part, oblivious to celestial events. They produce hair for a period ranging from two to six years, and then stop growing, apparently independent of all external or internal rhythms. So, while one shaft on your head may be growing, another may be shedding, and a third anchored and resting.

In 1926 at the University of Leeds, Professor Francis W. Dry, a skilled light microscopist, set out to describe the structure of hair follicles over the course of the cycle.[1] He found that although no new follicles arise during adult life, over time they change shape in fundamental and predictable ways. He likened these changes to the cyclic phases of the moon and gave them names.

"Anagen" is the name he gave to those follicles forming a new shaft. During this phase, the follicle projects into the deep skin, and the cells in its lowest portion divide at a blistering pace. As newly formed cells add to its base, the shaft moves toward and beyond the surface, about one half inch per month; the more time a follicle spends adding new cells to its base—that is, the more time it spends in the anagen phase—the longer the shaft becomes. Since scalp follicles remain in anagen for a period of two to six years, uncut human scalp hair may grow from one to three feet in length before shedding. Other hairs on different parts of the body are shorter because their anagen phase is not as long; eyelash hair, for example, grows only thirty days, and the resultant fiber is less than a half inch.[2]

As long as cells in the follicle base divide rapidly, the shaft will grow outward; however, when the shaft gets to a certain genetically determined length, the hair follicle stops producing hair shaft cells, the hair shaft stops moving outward, and the bottom of the follicle shrinks upward. Dry called this follicle-shrinkage phase "catagen." At this time, the follicle shortens because the cells making up its lower half shrivel up like raisins and disappear. What's fascinating about this shrinkage phase is that the lower follicle cells disappear in such a way that the follicle base withdraws in a bottom-to-top direction; the top of the follicle, however, does not change during the whole cycle, even as the shaft stops growing. By means of this life cycle, the hair follicle moves down and up, over and over, like a yo-yo, throughout a person's lifetime. As long as a person lives, his or her hair follicles will cycle in this way.[3]

Currently, scientists who study hair believe that very specific molecular signals tell the hair follicle when to start growing and when to stop growing and enter catagen. If we knew what those signals were, we would be able to turn hair growth off or on at will. Although we know little about these molecular keys, one study suggested a lead. Professor Gail Martin directs a laboratory at the University of California, San Francisco, that investigates the role of growth factors in mouse brain development.[4] In order to test the importance of any one factor, she and her team use genetic tools to generate mice lacking that factor. When the team removed one factor—fibroblast growth factor five—from all the cells in a group of mice, they discovered that the mice were perfectly healthy and had no nerve problems at all, but had very long coat hairs. In fact, these mice resembled angora animals such as angora guinea pigs, rabbits, goats, and cats, all of which have long, fine body hairs. When they studied the hair cycle phases of these mice, they found the mice had an abnormally long anagen phase; that long anagen phase produced abnormally long hair shafts. When these scientists looked for fibroblast growth factor five in other angora animals, they found much less than in normal-haired breeds. (A later study showed that a decrease of this factor in human hair follicles also results in very long hairs.[5]) Professor Martin and her colleagues concluded that this factor acts like an anagen brake regulating hair-shaft length. Currently, hair researchers are trying to find out how that factor works and if it can be used to treat hair disorders.

The catagen phase is short, lasting just a few days. At its end, the follicle enters a resting phase, which Professor Dry called "telogen," during which there is no cell growth, no cell division, and no shaft growth. In this phase, follicle length is the shortest, shaft length is longest, and shaft anchorage is strongest. That the resting phase can last from weeks to months is advantageous for furred animals living in cold habitats because, during the winter, protein-rich foods necessary for new shaft production may be limited. This resting phase finally ends when an anagen-stimulating growth factor signal arrives.

The fourth phase of the hair growth cycle is the phase of shedding, called "exogen." In this phase, hair-shaft mooring loosens and the shaft falls out. Because the hairless state is not viable for most mammals in the wild, there must be a delicate synchronization between shedding and new hair growth. Normally, exogen does not occur before a new hair shaft grows out. Studies suggest that shedding results when a battery of enzymes loosen the attachments holding the shaft in place. The rate of hair loss in humans is steady, with about fifty to one hundred scalp hairs falling out each day.

Control of the shedding phase is important because most of us don't care whether our hair is growing or resting, but when we sense we are shedding more hair than usual, we push the panic button.

Biologists have asked why hair follicles go through the bother of cycling. After all, except for the uterus (whose inner lining forms and sheds each month in a healthy menstruating woman), no other mature adult human organs cycle, form, cast off, and re-form. There must be an important survival reason for an organ to cycle, because building an organ and discarding it is expensive—costly in terms of the processes and resources needed both to build it up and tear it down. Three plausible explanations have been suggested. The first is based on the recognition that hair shafts wear down; even after such gentle handling as combing, shafts suffer structural damage. The second is that hair shedding provides animals a means of cleansing their coat, of exchanging a soiled cover for one free of dirt and vermin. The third explanation is that, through shedding, animals can adapt their fur coat to the changing habitat, such as when Minnesota weasels replace their sparse, brown summer coat for a dense, white winter coat. But why do humans shed hair? The simplest answer is that the cycle is part and parcel of hair growth itself—a remnant, or hand-me-down, of our distant past.

An abnormal hair cycle may have medical consequences. Following pregnancy, a woman may start shedding large quantities of scalp hair. That's because during pregnancy—when blood hormones necessary for development of a fetus are at high levels—the anagen phase is longer, and shedding is delayed, resulting in longer hair shafts and denser hair growth. After childbirth, when hormone levels return to normal, an unusually large number of hair follicles on the mother's scalp stop growing and enter the resting phase. Once a three-month resting phase is over, the hair shafts shed—in much larger quantities than most women have ever experienced.

Happily, in this case, by the time the old shafts shed, new hair fibers, though still rather short, have appeared.

Having recently given birth is a completely normal reason for any woman to undergo abundant shedding. But abnormal hair shedding may also occur as a result of other stressful life events, such as after general surgery, severe trauma, bereavement, divorce, and job loss. (We will revisit this phenomenon in the next chapter.) The fact that one can pinpoint a previous stressful event after three months (at the end of anagen, the follicle rests three months before shedding) reflects the remarkable consistency of the follicle's inherent clock.[6]

The hair cycle is also altered during cancer therapy. Once the diagnosis of breast cancer, for example, is established, the patient and her doctor choose from a number of different treatment options. In many cases the possible side effects may influence or even dictate the patient's ultimate treatment choice. During chemotherapy, the patient takes a cocktail of toxic drugs that kills all rapidly growing cells, both healthy and cancerous. The most actively dividing cells in the body are found in the bone marrow, intestine, and hair follicle base, and complaints of the patient receiving chemotherapy reflect injury to these tissues. She is weak and susceptible to infection because she lacks red blood and immune cells; she has abdominal cramps and diarrhea because of widespread injury to her gastrointestinal epithelial cell lining, and, most conspicuously, she has extensive hair loss because of damage to the rapidly growing cells in the lower hair follicle.

Using modern chemotherapy, we are not yet able to selectively destroy rapidly dividing cancer cells without injuring, at the same time, rapidly dividing normal cells. The hair follicle cycle is important to this discussion because telogen hair follicles, which house few dividing cells, are in fact resistant to chemotherapy:[7] They lack rapidly growing cells, the target of chemotherapy. The problem is that most scalp hair follicles are in the anagen phase and stay in anagen for years. Theoretically, if you could place hair follicles in the telogen phase during chemotherapy, you would minimize hair loss. We just don't know how to do that yet.

Once patients are off the anticancer drugs, all affected follicles undergo a well-deserved rest, and then reenter anagen to form a new shaft. However, the important hair follicle dividing cells have been destroyed, so how does the woebegone hair follicle reenter another cycle? This is where hair follicle stem cells come to the rescue.

In the years following World War II, Ludwig Auber obtained his PhD from the University of Edinburgh and joined the Wool Industries Research Association (now the British Textile Technology Group, Ltd), where he initiated a series of microscopic studies of the sheep hair follicle. Among many other fundamental observations, he documented that virtually all the rapidly growing cells of the hair follicle are located in a circumscribed region in the deepest portion. Other scientists in North America, Europe, Asia, and Australia confirmed Auber's observations and concluded that since most of the dividing cells are tucked into the lowest part of the follicle, the stem cells responsible for hair follicle cycling must be there as well.

This was the accepted wisdom until almost fifty years later, when George Cotsarelis challenged the convention. Cotsarelis knew that stem cells in other systems are very slow-growing reserve cells that have the unique ability to divide and form two daughter cells: One becomes a stem cell, like its parent, and the other becomes a cell that can form into one or more adult tissues, such as the hair follicle, its sebaceous gland, and the adjacent epidermis.[8]

Cotsarelis understood that if he could tag (in this case, the tag was a cell dye) all hair follicle cells at one time and then examine them weeks later, only the cells dividing at the slowest rate (that is, the stem cells) would retain the tag. This approach is based on the observation that when cells grow, they divide into equal halves, diluting the tag carried by the parent cell to one half in each of the daughter cells. Consider a teenager tippling her parents' vodka and then surreptitiously refilling the bottle with water each time the bottle reached half empty. By the sixth refill, the alcohol content would be below 1 percent, and no one—including her parents—would recognize the contents as anything even close to vodka; in fact, it would be more like pure water. The same dilution occurs for rapidly dividing cells in the deep follicle: As each cell divides at a rate of about twice per day, the dye tag becomes so diluted that by one week it is undetectable. On the other hand, cells that divide slowly, like stem cells, retain some of the initial tag even after a long period of time.

Using this approach, Cotsarelis carefully scrutinized the skin and its hair follicles for dye-retaining cells weeks after the skin cells had been tagged. Initially, he searched where his teachers told him to look—where all the action was, at the bottom of the follicle. But no tagged cells were there. Only when he moved his sights above the deep follicle—to the upper permanent portion of the hair follicle—did he discover his quarry. He found tagged cells clustered higher up in the anagen-phase follicle, at the point where the muscle of the hair follicle inserts. He reported to the scientific community that stem cells are located in the follicle mid-portion, a region referred to as the "bulge," not in its base.[9] The finding indicated that stem cells responsible for re-forming a new follicle after chemotherapy actually live in the mid-follicle, far away from the actively growing cells in the follicle base.

You might then assume that if you had a stem cell, all you would have to do is implant it anywhere in the skin and—*voilà!*—a new hair follicle would form with its stately shaft. But that's not what happens. Despite many attempts, when a pure population of these cells was placed into skin, no new hair follicles appeared. These experiments suggested that a second cell was needed to complete the task.

The story of that second cell takes us back across the Atlantic to the Firth of Tay, Scotland, where Professor Roy Oliver, an uprooted Englishman, had set up a laboratory at the University of Dundee to study the formation of organs, such as the tooth, liver, feather, and hair. At the time, during the 1960s, embryologists knew that the creation of most organs requires an interaction between two tissues: the epidermis and the dermis. Throughout the process of organ formation, these two tissues sit very close to each other and communicate, a conversation we listened to in the last chapter.

As wool scientists had previously found that hair follicles contain both epidermal and dermal portions, Oliver assumed these two tissues must play an important role in new hair follicle formation. He therefore chose to study the hair follicle as a model system for analyzing the dermal component of organ formation. In early studies, he found that if he removed the dermal papilla, a dense collection of dermal cells at the follicle base, hair growth stopped; when he transplanted it back, hair growth resumed. Moreover, in some eye-popping studies, when he and colleagues implanted a dermal papilla under the epidermis of rat skin, they found that the papilla had the embryonic power to induce hair follicles even in epidermis where none had existed before.[10]

To analyze how the dermal papilla works, Oliver assigned his then-graduate student Colin Jahoda to the project. Jahoda first established techniques for isolating dermal papillae from hair follicles, and then for growing dermal papilla cells in the laboratory. Eventually this team demonstrated that cells making up the dermal papilla can be propagated in the laboratory, and when the cells were injected back into the skin of a living mouse or rat, they had the power to induce new hair follicle formations. By means of multiple experiments, the Dundee group showed that the process of hair growth required a second important cell, and that that cell rests in the dermal papilla. When these dermal papilla cells interact with an intact epidermis, a full new hair follicle forms.

Because Cotsarelis could not get his epithelial stem cells to produce new hair follicles when implanted alone, he postulated that new hair follicle formation required an interaction between his unique epithelial stem cells and the dermal papilla cells Jahoda and Oliver had described. He also boldly proposed that the interaction between these two cell types is what drives hair to cycle. He believed that at the end of the resting phase, when epithelial stem cells and the dermal papilla cells are closest, they send conjugal messages to one another, which initiate a new cycle. In fact, when he and his colleagues planted these two cells into mouse skin, the combination formed new, cycling, shaft-producing hair follicles—a very dramatic result that suggested a new approach to the clinical problems of hair loss, a subject we will come back to.

While we believe we now know the main cellular actors in hair growth cycling—the upper follicle epithelial stem cells and the deeper dermal papilla cells—we do not yet understand how the cells communicate with one another; we know neither all the words of this cellular conversation nor exactly when or how loudly they are spoken. The current thought is that dermal cells in the follicle base send a message to the adjacent resting epithelial stem cells to initiate the anagen growth phase. The resting stem cells of the mid-follicle respond to the dermal signals by migrating down to replenish the dividing cells in the follicle base. The bottom portion of the follicle re-forms and then rebuilds a new shaft to launch the next cycle.

In the last decade, discoveries about the hair follicle cycle have stimulated research scientists to use the hair follicle as a model system for studying how stem cells do their job in regenerating other body parts. The hair follicle is an ideal model organ for studying regeneration, because it is readily available on the skin of all mammals, houses stem cells in a now-recognized region, and re-forms itself over and over again throughout the lifetime of the mammal. Scientists believe that knowledge acquired from the hair follicle will be directly applicable to re-forming organs essential to normal health, such as the tooth, kidney, liver, brain, eye, finger, and skin.

But the hair follicle is not an island. Changes in the body from which it grows impact hair just as rain and soil conditions affect a corn crop. Emotional stresses can cause scalp hairs to go white, and body hormones can cause scalps to go bald. These kinds of anomalies can lead to truly bad hair days—and can teach us even more about our own hair.

4

INFLUENTIAL NEIGHBORS

The stress of prolonged sound reduces hair growth.

I n his short story "Descent into the Maelstrom," Edgar Allan Poe describes the story of a young fisherman who was trawling far off the Norwegian coast when suddenly the skies darkened and the seas rose. As the fisherman turned his boat homeward, the surrounding waters gathered into a gigantic whirlpool. Although he was a veteran sailor, he couldn't steer clear of the spiraling waters that drew his boat closer and closer to the steep black funnel. In the struggle, the fisherman lost his companion and boat, but he lived to tell the narrator, "You suppose me a very old man—but I am not. It took less than a single day to change these hairs from a jetty black to white . . . Those who drew me on board were my old mates and daily companions—but they know me no more than they would have known a traveler from the spirit-land. My hair, which had been raven black the day before, was as white as you see it now."

The story is fictional, but the dramatic change Poe described was likely based on something Poe either saw himself or heard rumor of. On rare occasions, physicians have observed that a horrendous emotional and life-threatening shock can cause a sudden hair change.

Environmental events lead to body responses of all kinds. During a movie, for example, we react to humorous, sad, or threatening scenes with laughter, tears, or rapid pulse. So what, exactly, happened to the fisherman?

The most likely explanation is that he started the day with a mixture of white and dark, salt-and-pepper hair but lost the colored shafts as a result of an underlying disorder triggered by the fright. The selective shedding of dark hairs could unmask a white scalp. Contemporary dermatologists would diagnose him with the sudden onset of *alopecia areata*.

Alopecia areata is not a rare disease: It affects about two out of every one hundred people. Though it usually causes hair loss in a small, discrete area of skin, it can also cause loss of all head hair or all body hair. The fisherman probably had early hair graying before the maelstrom and the life-threatening shock triggered latent alopecia areata, which caused his black hair shafts to shed, leaving his scalp "as white as you see it now."

The life-threat that the fisherman suffered sent an all-hands-on-deck message throughout his body. His other body organs and tissues responded when stress signals reached them (e.g., rapid pulse, increased blood pressure, decreased appetite) and when those signals arrived in the skin, they directed the hair follicles to shed their colored shafts on the double. The signals that precipitated hair shaft shedding (that is, the perceived threat of the maelstrom) did not initiate within the hair follicle itself; they arose from elsewhere in the body. In alopecia areata, the problem is not with the hair follicle, either; the follicle can grow and cycle. The illness is with the body, which views the hair follicle as a *persona non grata*, as a native structure needing restraint. The body sends the immune system—its cells and antibodies—to do the dirty work. The alopecia areata hair follicle continues to grow but its cycle reaches only the earliest phase of anagen before an immune attack blocks it. Although follicles try to grow over and over again, as long as the disease persists, neither full anagen nor new hair shafts form.

How did the near-death experience reach the fisherman's follicles? After all, his eyes, ears, and body experienced the threat, not his hair follicles. Ralf Paus, a professor on the faculties of the University of Manchester and the University of Muenster, has spent his career studying the influences of surrounding tissues on hair follicle health. In general, his work indicates that what's going on in the body can affect hair growth. In 2003, Paus and his colleagues posited that if stress affects hair follicles, it should be demonstrable under controlled conditions. To test their hypothesis, they exposed adult mice to short pulses of surround sound (middle A, 400 hertz) every fifteen seconds for twenty-four hours. While not as bad as elevator music, this sound was enough of an irritant to reduce the number of pups a pregnant dam carried to term. The researchers found that the stress impacted the hair follicle, too, imposing a brake on the hair growth cycle: Anagen stopped and the follicles entered catagen. But how did this acoustic annoyance reach the hair follicle? Paus and his colleagues believed that the stress could have traveled by way of hormones or nerves and so, in their experiments, they blocked the skin nerves and found that they also blocked the stress effect. In this way, they showed that stress can reproducibly affect hair health and that nerves can transmit stress signals to hair.[1]

Whereas sound stress can inhibit hair growth, it's been found that wounding—a direct injury from the outside—can actually stimulate it. If hair follicles or the skin around them are injured (such as by a cut), a new hair shaft will form—not a new hair follicle, a new hair shaft.[2] Injury will wake up a telogen follicle to enter anagen and, in anagen, a new shaft will form, essentially identical to the one lost. Unlike the response of noise-stressed mice, though, the injury response occurs whether or not the surrounding nerves are functional. Scientists are not entirely sure why the follicle reacts to injury in this way. What we are certain about, though, is that hair shafts themselves play no role in orchestrating a wound response because the cells making up the shaft are not living. They can't eat, feel, or grow and they lack blood vessels and nerves; hair shaft cells are essentially fossilized. So gently cutting a hair shaft, such as during routine barbering or leg shaving, is a clandestine affair between you and the scissors; neither the hair follicle nor the body will ever know. Yet if in the course of barbering, you give the shafts a series of hard yanks, or pluck them out, follicles will perceive an injury and respond with a full anagen phase and new shaft.

But the hair follicle neighborhood contains more than nerves. It sits in skin, a juicy milieu of hormones, chemicals, and growth factors, some deposited by the blood and others generated by local cells. The blood-borne hormones arise from endocrine organs, which include the pituitary gland (located at the bottom of the brain), adrenal gland (which sits on top of the kidneys), thyroid gland (attached to the windpipe in the neck), and sex organs. A surprising result is that all these organs produce hormones that affect hair follicle growth in one way or another.[3]

The role of a hormone is best illustrated by what happens in its absence. One example is hypothyroidism, a condition in which the patient doesn't have enough thyroid hormone to go around. Recognized as early as Roman times and referred to as cretinism in the 18th century, its symptoms include sluggishness, mental deficiency, puffy skin, and thinned, bristly hair. While physicians recognized these findings as a syndrome, they did not realize until the early 19th century that the problem was due to a nonfunctioning thyroid gland. And although nowadays physicians diagnose hypothyroidism in a baby at birth, spotting it in adults has always been more difficult, because the symptoms evolve slowly. Sir William Gull, Queen Victoria's physician, recognized the onset of adult hypothyroidism in his paper entitled "On a Cretinoid State Supervening in Adult Life in Women."[4] The patients become "more and more languid," he wrote. "Skin becomes thick and folded . . . The hair is flaxen and soft" and becomes coarse, brittle, and strawlike. Hypothyroidism is accompanied by hair loss in scalp, underarm, and pubic areas. Although we don't know the precise role thyroid hormone plays in hair health, we know in its absence, cell metabolism is abnormal, hair follicle cycling is shortened, and the shafts that form are stiff and breakable.

Androgens—male-forming hormones, which are blood-borne in both sexes—also affect the maturation of most body hair follicles, though follicles in different regions respond differently. Hair follicles along the sides of the scalp are completely insensitive to blood androgens; these follicles grow and produce a shaft regardless of blood androgen concentration. In contrast, follicles of the underarm or pubic regions start to enlarge when androgens are in low concentration, so in early adolescence, with the first surge of blood androgens, coarse hairs appear in the pubic region and then later in the underarm and on the leg.

In the young male, as androgen levels rise still further, the small hairs on his face and chest enlarge. Androgens are important to body hair growth in women as well, but, because their circulating levels normally remain low, coarse body hairs are not a female thing. The examining physician looks for androgen-sensitive hairs in diagnosing patient health. Lack of body hair growth in males may alert the physician to testicular dysfunction. The presence of long and coarse body hairs in adult women may alert the physician to androgen-producing tumors arising in the ovary or adrenal gland.

Androgen molecules act on small follicles of maturing adolescent skin by binding to cells in the follicle base and initiating a message that tells the follicles to change because they are no longer juvenile and thus must broadcast adulthood. Though hair follicle cells don't make androgens, they do make molecules that receive, recognize, accept, and interpret the androgen message. Moreover, they have the wherewithal to process the arriving androgens by either enhancing or reducing their activity. The ability of hair follicles to modify circulating androgens explains the varying hormone sensitivity of different hair follicles.

Perhaps the most widespread dysfunction of hair is male pattern baldness. It usually starts within the third or fourth decade of life, but may start in adolescence after sexual maturity. It's an inherited condition striking some families more than others, coursing down the paternal line in some families and the maternal line in others. Hair loss is extremely common; in fact, among North American males, one half of the population shows some degree of balding by the age of fifty.

Male pattern balding[5] has been a part of the human experience as long as man has been a species. Egyptian papyrus scripts dating back four thousand years record that hair loss has concerned most bald males—even the powerful ones. One historic example is the successful general, statesman, and first absolute ruler of the Roman Empire, Julius Caesar, who was so concerned with his shiny pate that he tried to cover it up. As the Roman historian Suetonius describes in *The Lives of the Twelve Caesars*: "His baldness was a disfigurement which troubled him greatly, since he found that it was often the subject of the gibes of his detractors. Because of it he used to comb forward his scanty locks from the crown of his head."[6]

Though we understand the word "bald" to suggest skin without hair, it is, in fact, a misnomer. A "bald" head has plenty of hair follicles and hair shafts, but they are frightfully small, only microscopically visible. The mechanism of balding involves the progressive miniaturization of the hair follicle and its shaft: As the disease progresses, the hair follicle and its shaft get smaller and smaller with each cycle.

But how does that large, normal follicle turn into a small one? The suspicion that male hormones play a role in male pattern baldness is at least as old as Aristotle (who stated "eunuchs, too, [like women] do not go bald"),[7] but scientists were long unable to prove it. Even as physicians became aware of the role of hormones in disease in the early part of the 20th century, they found themselves with a major problem: There were no animals that produced a reliable model of human balding that they could study in the lab. As a result, human patients were needed. The ideal patient would be a man with very low circulating androgens (similar to the study of thyroid hormone in patients with hypothyroidism), but these patients weren't exactly easy to find.

A solution surfaced in 1942, when James Hamilton, a professor of anatomy at Yale University School of Medicine who had a long-term interest in male pattern balding, found a group of 104 castrated men.[8] These men all had very low blood androgen concentration, and they made for ideal study subjects because within this group some of the men had been castrated before adolescence, some during adolescence, and others later in life. Those subjects castrated before adolescence had no mature male characteristics; they showed scant body hair, no beard, undeveloped sexual organs and, significantly, no male pattern balding. When these men were given injections of androgen, not only did they acquire mature male body features, greater muscles, and enlarged sex organs, but those with a family history of balding also became bald. (Needless to say, this kind of experiment could not be done today.) The study demonstrated two aspects of male pattern balding: first, that androgens are necessary and, second, that there must be a genetic basis—a bald father or grandfather. (Lest anyone get any ideas, Hamilton also noted that men who were castrated *after* they started to go bald did not regrow their hair once their androgen levels dropped; once balding occurs, reducing androgen levels—even to the drastic level of castration—will not reverse hair loss.[9])

The study was groundbreaking, but Hamilton's research didn't stop there. He next turned his attention to the specific patterns of baldness. In fact, these patterns are so predictable that Hamilton was able to propose in 1951 that all balding males could be classified into one of eight types; the balding patterns ranged from one with a high forehead to one with a shiny spot in the skull cap area to one almost completely bald (except for hair around the temples).[10]

The fascinating thing about balding is that it doesn't occur everywhere; it's unique to the scalp, and even there it only affects the crown—not the side of the scalp or the beard areas. Follicle location is important to this form of hair loss; we're just still not sure why.[11]

We do know, however, that healthy hair requires a healthy body. Because the hair follicle requires ample resources to produce a shaft, how it grows is a reliable indicator of overall body fitness.

As the hair follicle houses some of the most rapidly growing cells of the body, it must be well fed. One example of the impact of malnutrition on hair occurs in developing countries where there are inadequate dietary proteins; after all, hair is mostly protein. That's what we see with malnourished children, whose stick-thin arms and legs and bulging bellies are accompanied by thin, curly, discolored, brittle, and slow-growing hair. But hair shaft abnormalities due to nutrition are not limited to developing countries. In dermatology clinics in industrialized countries, it is not unusual for dieting women to present with hair problems. A woman on an iron-poor diet can become anemic enough to experience not only weakness, fatigue, and dizziness, but also hair loss. Fortunately, the anemia and hair loss are easily treated with iron supplements, and new hair growth will appear within several months after starting supplements.

Proper nutrition is a big deal for sheep, too. Consider that a merino ewe makes about twelve pounds of pure wool per year. In order to produce this amount of wool, a sheep will have to consume at least three and a half ounces of pure protein per day. (Lactating ewes require even more.) Because grass is a rather poor protein source, sheep must consume at least nine pounds of fresh pasture per day; for them, grazing is an all-day job.

Upon a healthy body, lush hair will grow. For most animals, abundant hair provides a barrier to the threats and inconsistencies of the surroundings. Modern humans don't need hair as a shield. For us, hair has become important in other ways.

PART TWO

~

THE ULTIMATE COMMUNICATOR

5

ENKIDU CUTS HIS HAIR

———

Hair sends serious messages and can invoke surprisingly emotional reactions: In early 20th-century China, modernization efforts forced men to cut their traditional queues. In defense of this long-held and venerated hairstyle, many in the countryside committed murder or suicide.

T he link between hair and beauty has always been strong, but the issue of its absence would be broached at the Mrs. Washington International Beauty Queen Contest in 1997 with a shocking revelation. As pageant winner Cari Bickley moved to center stage, the audience applauded her confident walk, bright, communicative eyes, and well-proportioned body. Once at the podium, Bickley brushed her hand along her flowing auburn hair. She drew back her hand, as if to sweep her hair from her face, and away it fell—all of it. The beauty queen was bald![1] "I wanted to send a message," Bickley said after the event. "Who you are is far more important than what you look like."[2]

Two years earlier, Bickley had entered the same contest without a wig—and left without the crown. Bickley's story underscores the truism that physical beauty—of the Miss or Mrs. America type—is inseparable from hair, and that the social messages sent by a full head of hair are worlds apart from those sent by a bald scalp.

Cari Bickley has alopecia areata,[3] a hair-loss condition that afflicts about two out of every hundred Americans and can strike a member of any ethnic group at any age. In its most common form, it manifests as coin-shaped patches of hair loss wherever hair would normally be present: the scalp, eyebrows, eyelashes, arms, legs, wherever. In mild forms of the disease, hair regrowth usually occurs after therapeutic steroid injections and can even happen spontaneously without any treatment. In any event, with mild cases, the hair-loss areas are so small that the patient is generally able to cover the spaces cosmetically.

In the more severe forms of alopecia areata, however, the patient loses most of her hair very quickly. It's not unusual for the affected person to wake up one morning and find large clumps of scalp hair lying on her pillow. Physicians find that a person with widespread hair loss experiences the same reaction as anyone who has lost an important body part, such as an arm or leg. That person undergoes the emotionally painful stages of loss—denial, anger, bargaining, depression, and acceptance—described by Elizabeth Kübler-Ross.

Each person adjusts to the condition in his or her own unique way. Some people accept their hair loss boldly, willing to face the world without hair, whatever the consequences. For example, Richard M. Rosenblum, former chairman of the New York State Republican Party from 1972 to 1977 and an adviser to Governor Nelson Rockefeller, enjoyed a brilliantly successful political career living with total hair loss. Another example is Angela Christiano, PhD, currently a professor of dermatology, genetics, and development at Columbia University, who not only came to terms with her own hair loss but also decided to do something about it by redirecting the research of her laboratory to identify the genetic cause of alopecia and seek its treatments. At the other end of the spectrum are people unwilling to face the world without some sort of head cover; they either withdraw from society or put on a wig. One such person was the first John D. Rockefeller, who lost all of his hair—scalp, eyelashes, eyebrows, and body hair—when he was in his midfifties.[4] Pictures in his senior years show the tycoon with a rather ill-fitting, white-haired wig, giving him plenty of hair on top but none on his temples, brows, or lashes. For most people, individual acceptance comes with time, simply by living without hair, and by sharing experiences with those similarly affected.[5]

With her unexpected disclosure, beauty queen Bickley put into focus the importance of hair in human life: the ability to send messages from person to person as well as from individual to group. The person without hair lacks one of the most important tools servicing interpersonal communication, a device that acts both nonverbally and often at a distance.

We create the unspoken messages we send to each other every day from those bodily components we can mold—body movements, facial expressions, nails, and hair. Hair sends signals from wherever on the body it grows—head, face, armpit, groin, and to a lesser extent chest, arms, and legs—but the most important sites are the scalp, eyebrows, eyelashes, and beard. We craft messages by shaping hair—leaving it long, cutting it, curling it, straightening it, coloring it, or even removing it altogether. Furthermore, we embellish hair by placing adornments over, upon, or within it, such as wigs, hats, pins, pillows, trinkets, and frames—but that is a topic we will return to in a later chapter.

For behavioral zoologists, interpreting the exact message a specific hair arrangement—or for that matter, a feather arrangement—sends has been difficult and often uncertain at best. Since birds use feathers in mating rituals, it is reasonable to assume that feather messages influence mating success. But with few scientific studies carried out to define messages in terms of habitat, camouflage, and interspecies communication in either animals or humans, their meanings are largely assumed and must be extrapolated from behavioral consequences. In his book *Ornithology*, published in 1995, Frank B. Gill of the Academy of Natural Sciences in Philadelphia writes, "Deciphering the information transmitted by a [feather] display remains one of the greatest challenges in the study of bird behavior. Ornithologists can only guess at the message of a display from correlations between preceding and succeeding actions of sender and receiver."

Considering the role of feathers in avian mating habits, it's equally reasonable to assume that mammals use hair to communicate. One example is the fur flare of the family cat: an indisputable message of aggression to whomever is around. In a study of the African lion, professors Peyton West and Craig Packer of the University of Minnesota observed that the male lion successfully uses his mane to send mating and social messages. They reported that female lions of the Serengeti National Park preferred males sporting heavily pigmented manes, and that males endowed with dark and long-haired manes enjoyed a greater dominance over the male community.[6]

Similarly, the messages humans send by means of hair are not always so easy to determine, and objective research is rarely undertaken to characterize them. Complicating the interpretation of any specific hair arrangement are the cultural, historical, and environmental backgrounds of the sender and the receiver. For example, how can anyone measure, let alone know for certain, whether blondes have more fun? Would they still have more fun in a society that prizes dark-haired beauty? Or consider eyelashes: Our society admires them lengthy and curled, but when is an eyelash too long to be sexy? And beards: At what point do beard hairs transit from distinguished to unkempt? And hair color: When does gray hair connote experience and wisdom and when does it imply old age and irrelevance? The interpretation of these nonverbal messages is critical because messages elicit action.

Despite the uncertainty in interpretation, it's uncanny how often people in different regions, cultures, and periods react to similar hairstyles the same way. If we draw an analogy with animal behavior, it's reasonable to assume that the messages humans send to one another by means of hair are also hardwired in our genes. The messages are emotionally charged,[7] and, as suggested by anthropologists, historians, psychologists, and cosmetologists, they fall into several categories: self-identification, humanness, social-sexual fitness, and religion.

"Blondie," "Curly," "Baldy," "Skinhead," "Hairy," "Carrot-top," and "Rusty" are hair-based monikers used to identify people. For example, historical record tells us Erik the Red, who founded the first western settlement in Greenland in 985 c.e., was not only a successful seafaring leader and a renegade but also a bearer of bright red hair. When the 10th-century Norwegian prince Harald Halfdansson vowed to let his hair grow until he conquered all of Norway, his followers gave him the name Harald Tanglehair. In due course, he united the country, true to his pledge, and on becoming king, he assumed a new title: Harald I Fairhair. The story behind the name of Charles the Bald, the Holy Roman Emperor and king of West Francia from 840 to 877 C.E., on the other hand, is less clear. Some scholars believe that the cognomen refers to Charles's landlessness rather than to his glabrous pate, while others think it was an account of his appearance. In either case, throughout history people used hair descriptors to label and tell us something about their kings.

Great writers, bards, and other narrators use hair to identify and give personality to their characters. In *The Fellowship of the Ring*, Tolkien distinguished the hobbits and dwarfs in part by their hair patterning: hobbits, for example, are depicted with furry feet but no facial hair. In the Gothic legend of Bluebeard there lived a mysterious count known for his dark blue-black beard and vanishing wives. In his cold, gloomy, dank, and desolate castle, he warned each of his wives—a series of six—not to look behind a locked door, even though he gave each of them the key. When he discovered that, despite his command, his wives entered the secret room, he murdered them. His full black beard signaled maleficence and alerts us to stay away. In contrast, in a very different location and story, the bushy, white, grandfatherly beard of Santa Claus invites us to snuggle up.

Even today, we identify famous people by their hair. In fact, the graphic artist Christina Christoforou has shown that black pen sketches of hair alone—without facial features or clothes—can be enough for the viewer to recognize a person. Head-hair silhouettes of Abraham Lincoln, Ronald Reagan, and Margaret Thatcher, for example, are unequivocally revealing. For Christoforou, "a feature as trivial as hairstyle becomes part of that person's identity and why we recognize them. In my eyes, Jimi Hendrix's hairstyle says 'freedom' [and] Audrey Hepburn's 'elegance.'"[8] On an everyday level, it is often befuddling, humbling, and embarrassing to misidentify or even overlook friends who have changed their hair or beard styles. Take, for example, a young child who doesn't recognize her father after he shaves his long beard.

Although we tend to believe the way we style our hair today is unique and novel, in fact the same or similar hairstyles have been used over and over again, extending as far back as ancient Egypt. While the time elapsed between the cycle of a given hairstyle may range from years to centuries, its reprise is as predictable as a full moon.[9]

The cyclic nature of styles is shown just by looking at men's fashion in the United States over the last two hundred years. Take the subject of beards. At the outset of the 19th century, sporting a full beard was considered socially unacceptable and, in some places, outright distasteful. During this era, a man grew a beard at great personal risk. One well-known beard wearer was Joseph Palmer, veteran of the War of 1812 and ardent abolitionist.[10] Because of his unconventional insistence on wearing a bushy gray beard, he was taunted and even physically abused. In 1830, he was attacked in Fitchburg, New York, by a group of men who took it upon themselves to debeard him. When Palmer drew a knife in defense, he was arrested and jailed for defending his beard. A mission-driven, recalcitrant, and impetuous fellow, Palmer never did remove his beard. However, before the end of his life, he enjoyed some degree of vindication, since by the mid-19th century, facial hair had come back into fashion once more, and most men adopted bushy sideburns, mustaches, and beards.

The truth is, except for Andrew Johnson, all U.S. presidents of the late 19th century wore a prominent beard or mustache, while keeping their scalp hair short. Lincoln switched from clean-shaven to bearded, apparently because of a letter he received in 1860 from Grace Bedell, an eleven-year-old girl from Westfield, New York. She wrote the presidential candidate: "If you let your whiskers grow I will try and get the rest of them [my brothers] to vote for you, you would look a great deal better for your face is so thin." Lincoln replied to her on October 19, 1860: "As to the whiskers have never worn any do you not think people would call it a silly affection if I would to begin it now?"[11] In February 1861, displaying a three-month beard growth, Lincoln met Bedell in person and credited her for the suggestion. With the advent of the 20th century, men at last adopted clean-shaven cheeks but kept their mustaches. It wasn't until the 1960s that beards returned in a big way. And, still, they went back out of fashion by the 1980s, only to return with a vengeance with the modern hipster.

Men's hairstyles can be viewed in the same way. During the American Revolution, minutemen wore their hair pretty much as they pleased, which generally meant long and unbound. In 1780, George Washington felt the army needed a smarter, more disciplined look, and ordered his men to be "shaved, combed and powdered."[12] By the early 1800s, young men were cutting their hair short to distinguish themselves from gentlemen of the old order who still powdered their hair and wore it in queues. Two decades later, these young men were offended when their own sons chose to distinguish themselves from the "older" generation by letting their hair grow long and sometimes curling it into ringlets. By the end of the 19th century, short hair had returned to fashion. The trend continued in the mid-1940s, when Yanks coming home from World War II brought with them the "butch" or "crew" cut. Some men even shaved their heads completely, following the example of actor Yul Brynner after his 1951 performance in *The King and I*. In the late 1960s, however, the trend for growing hair longer returned under the influence of Elvis Presley, the Beatles, and the counterculture of that era. The early 1990s brought a wide variety of styles all at once: Long hair, short hair, sideburns, mustaches, and beards were equally acceptable in most circles as long as the presentations were neatly groomed. Since then, the Yul Brynner hairless fashion returned, as demonstrated by celebrities Bruce Willis, LL Cool J, Pitbull, Dwayne "The Rock" Johnson, and Vin Diesel. Now, men with a completely shaved scalp pride themselves on a newfound prepossession and sexiness in the bald look.[13]

Trends in women's hair also repeat. In the American colonies of the 1700s, hairstyles for women mirrored those in Europe with hair powdered, pinned up quite short in the back, and curled in the front. Although most young women wore long hair styled in braids or hanging loose, in the 1890s, a more insouciant style appeared, associated with the first pinup, the Gibson Girl, painted by Charles Dana Gibson. She swept her hair up into a soft, puffy pompadour rolled from temple to temple over a horsehair pillow. With her cloudlike hairdo, society viewed her as independent, self-assured, strong-willed, and worthy of respect. About the same time, Marcel's curling iron gave women the opportunity to place well-formed waves in their bobbed hair. Following World War I, as women assumed more responsibility outside the home, they preferred shorter hairstyles; by the end of the 1920s, millions of women of all ages wore short hair. Long hairstyles returned in the 1940s, influenced by such celebrities as Hollywood actress Veronica Lake with her seductive tress and Mamie Eisenhower with her signature bangs. In the 1950s, the short haircut of Audrey Hepburn transitioned to the bouffant of Jacqueline Kennedy and the ubiquitous long hair of teenage ponytails. Once again, short playboy hair appeared in the 1960s and long, feathered hairdos like Farrah Fawcett's in the 1970s.[14]

Historically, these same styles appear and disappear over time, enjoying a short period of popularity, a rapid demise, and, sometime later, a renaissance associated with all the delights of something "new." A given hairstyle tends to label one generation but not the one immediately before or after, since they're mostly reactionary. Not surprisingly, generations often clash over music and hairstyles. In the past, religious leaders often railed against new hairstyles and labeled them morally improper, a threat to the salvation of souls. In the late 18th century, for example, New England clergy expressed displeasure over the high-piled hairstyles of young girls. Manasseh Cutler, a Yale-trained pastor, claimed in 1781 that the new hairstyle reminded him of "the monstrous . . . devil."[15] So, by this decree, long hair heaped high was God-cursed. Yet 130 years later, in the 1910s, it was short hair that was considered morally objectionable: At a time when most women were bobbing their hair, preachers warned that short hair was seductive and therefore implied, if not directly indicated, the existence of serious negative moral predispositions.

Over and over again in legend, art, and history, people have used hair to distinguish human from animal, citizen from savage, neighbor from foreigner, friend from adversary. In the Babylonian legend of Gilgamesh, the goddess Anruru "moistened her hands, she pinched off some clay, she threw it into the wilderness, kneaded it, shaped it to her idea, and fashioned a man, a warrior, a hero, Enkidu the brave, as powerful and fierce as the war god Ninurta. Hair covered his body, hair grew thick on his head and hung down to his waist, like a woman's hair." In the legend, this newly created man-hero was as ferocious and wild as the animals with whom he lived. So when the shepherds in the neighborhood became concerned for their safety, they approached their king, Gilgamesh, who recommended the help of "a woman named

Shamhat, one of the priestesses who give their bodies to any man, in honor of the goddess [Ishtar who] . . . used her love arts, she took his breath with her kisses, held nothing back, and showed him what a woman is. For seven days he stayed erect and made love with her."[16] At the end of this arduous trial, what did our hero do? He "had his hair cut"! By "taming" his hair, Enkidu declared his conversion from a terrifying, uncouth, and unpredictable savage to a responsible individual. Through this gesture, he demonstrated that he was now civilized, so much so that he became a close friend of Gilgamesh, the king.

In the Bible, we see the hairless man as the chosen one, a figure of elevated status among his people. In the Old Testament, the hairless man Jacob, a "plain man" living in a tent, steals the birthright and blessings from his brother Esau, "a skillful hunter, a man of the field . . . a hairy man." According to the story, hair served as a key component distinguishing the God-favored Jacob from the less-favored Esau. Not only does Jacob, the hairless, get away with the canard, but he lives to father the Twelve Tribes of Israel.

For Romans of the Classical era, a barbarian was one of the wild-haired people of the distant and beyond, who were foreign to them in culture, language, and dress. These barbarians, including the Germans and Celts, often displayed long, unkempt scalp and facial hair,[17] which contrasted sharply with the well-trimmed city-dwellers of the Mediterranean littoral.

During the late Imperial period from the 17th century to the 21st century, Chinese philosophers contended that humanness (as defined as cultural features separating *Homo sapiens* from animals, such as history, art, law, and an absence of cannibalism) was inversely related to the quantity of hair growing on a person's body. They argued that, because dense body hair was a feature of primitive animals, the amount of body hair on any creature determined its status in the animal kingdom. As they naturally exhibit little body hair, scant male beard, no chest hair, and variable pubic hair, the Chinese of this era viewed hairy people as uncivilized—if, in fact, they could be characterized as people at all. So, when the bearded and generally hairy Europeans arrived on their shores in the 16th and 17th centuries, the Chinese were confused and reluctant to accept them as equals.

Just as hair has been used to express, advertise, or instill humanity and civilization, it has also been used, conversely and perversely, to dehumanize. It is, and has been, the custom of governmental authorities, for example, to shave head hair off convicted criminals before execution. Before Joan of Arc was burned at the stake in May 1431, her executioners shaved her head. So was it with the aristocracy as well: Anne Boleyn, second wife to Henry VIII, had her head shaved before her beheading by sword in 1536, as did Marie Antoinette before she faced the guillotine in 1793. During Hitler's Final Solution in World War II, the Jews and others arriving at Auschwitz had their body hair shaven off at the same time they were registered, tattooed, and deloused. They also had their heads shaven clean prior to execution. In January 1945, when the Soviet troops liberated Auschwitz, they found seven tons of human hair. While this act was certainly meant to dehumanize, in this society human hair also had economic value: A cloth company paid fifty pfennig per kilo for it.[18] On the other side of this conflict, in post–World War II France, women accused of collaborating with Nazis were paraded through the cities with fully shaven scalps. African slave traders, too, shaved the heads of their human chattel before transporting them to the New World.[19] Even today, when capital punishment is administered by electrocution, the felon's head is shaved, allegedly to optimize electrode-to-skin contact. The executioners lamely justify shaving as a matter of efficiency, cleanliness, and so on; nevertheless, the act sends an undeniable message of dehumanization and domination.

Hair also sends messages about body health, strength, and sexuality. Hair loss, for example, is often equated with serious illness. In general, this perception is wrong. The most common forms of hair loss—such as male pattern balding, female hair thinning, hair loss after pregnancy, and alopecia areata—don't indicate anything detrimental to one's overall health. However, some infectious diseases do have hair loss as a side-effect. In the condition *tinea capitis* (scalp ringworm), a fungus attacks the hair of elementary school children, resulting in hairless, red, scaly, moist, and pustular scalp patches. Another example, mange, results from the infestation of a parasitic mite that lives on skin and hair, causing severe itching and hair shedding. What results from this infection can be easily confused with alopecia areata. (In fact, the word "alopecia" derives from the Greek word for fox, *alopex*, because the ancients equated the hair loss seen in mange-affected foxes to the patchy hair loss seen in humans with the common form of alopecia areata.) Because there are so many hair-follicle diseases with varied presentations, one can see how people unfamiliar with the whole gamut of hair-loss disorders might confuse the noninfectious with the infectious. Such is the dilemma people with longstanding hair loss must face.

In contrast, lush, full hair growth sends signals of robust health, personal attractiveness, and active sexuality. In an Asian-Indian hymn, a young girl prays to the Hindu god Indra—ruler of the heavens and god of thunder and rain—to make hair grow on her father's head, hair grow on her pubic region, and crops grow in her father's fields, thus associating the procreation of the fields with health and reproduction of human life.[20]

In many cultures, fine, loose, long hair denotes receptive female sexuality. In Japanese society, for example, long black hair of the female has historically been equated to life force, sexual energy, growth, and fertility.[21] Long, healthy hair symbolizing sexual receptivity is also recorded in European folk myth. In the original story of Rapunzel, written by the Brothers Grimm, a beautiful girl with long, flowing hair is confined to a tower. The girl's unusually lengthy hair gives the wicked sorceress access to the prisoner, but it also attracts and facilitates the tryst with a handsome prince—that legendary hair quite literally begets a sexual encounter for Rapunzel with resultant twin babies in tow.

Although the most important hair messages come from head hair (because that is what we most commonly see), body hair also sends its own messages. Global body hair is a common male attribute and is generally tolerated on a male body—anywhere and everywhere, short or long.[22] For the female, though, body hair is a different matter, and women of many eras have gone to great lengths to banish any hairs beyond those of a prepubescent girl. Modern women certainly know the experience of being plucked, waxed, and lasered, but it's hardly a new phenomenon. In 1486, Botticelli captured the idealized body in his painting *The Birth of Venus*—the image of a sexually mature goddess, utterly hairless besides long, attractive tresses flowing from her scalp.

Covering what it does, pubic hair has its own story. Growing about the genitals and crotch area, this hair may be sparse, thick, fine, or coarse depending on the individual; it is generally more darkly pigmented than hair elsewhere. A lot of emotional energy centers around this hair as if its exposure is a sign for action, so it is hardly surprising that revealing it is generally restricted in most cultures. Some cultures, such as ancient Egypt and Greece and modern Muslims, advocate its complete removal because the hair is considered uncivilized or unclean. In the United States, one survey showed 90 percent of modern fashion-conscious women trim or remove their pubic hair.[23] In other cultures, full pubic hair is a *sine qua non*—you must have it, but you can't show it.[24] In modern-day Korea, pubic hair is so important to the life of some women that cosmetic surgeons transplant hairs (usually from the scalp) in order to bush up this well-hidden zone.[25]

Contradictions regarding pubic hair may be incorporated into regulatory policies. Up until recently, censorship laws in Japan restricted the display of woman's pubic hair in any art form. At that time, movie directors had to tiptoe between aesthetic sexual messages and the hypersensitive licensing authorities. To be sure, there was an odor of inconsistency, even hypocrisy, in the regulatory policy enforced here, given Japan's depiction of women. In her essay "Cutting the Fringes: Pubic Hair at the Margins of Japanese Censorship Laws," Professor Anne Allison contends: "In a country where pictures of naked women appear in news magazines, naked breasts in public advertisements, scenes of rape and nudity on television and sado-masochistic scenarios in comic books . . . pubic hair is notably absent in a popular culture of constant and graphic sexual images."[26]

At least up to the early 20th century, Western artists have treated pubic hair with a disciplined respect. Classical sculpture and graphic creations either show no genital hair or stylized renditions. It took modern artists such as Pablo Picasso and Egon Schiele to lift the fig leaves and depict the region as nature has it.

Hair arrangement often reveals the position of a person in society; for example, hairstyle may indicate stages of life. In Kathmandu, for example, young women keep their hair short and straight by cutting it every few months. Approaching marriageable age, as early as fifteen or sixteen years old, they grow their hair long. At marriage, their hair is shoulder length or longer, but in public it is bound in a bun. Older women with grown children once again cut their hair short.[27]

Grandiosity of hairstyle telegraphs status, power, and wealth in most societies. This generalization is based on the fact that hair ornamentation takes time and at least one servant to complete. Even in more primitive cultures, such as those in South Central Africa where elaborate dressing of the hair is prized, only the chiefs or high-ranking dignitaries with the necessary power and wealth can afford the intricate braided or bundled hairstyles featuring entwined beads and diadems.[28]

A shaved scalp may reflect political power. In ancient Egypt, noblemen shaved their scalps completely except for one long lock recognized as a sign of majesty. In a somewhat different form, noblewomen of 14th- to 16th-century Europe and England shaved or plucked their frontal scalp in order to create a prominent forehead: Elizabeth I, the great virgin queen, appears so in extant portraits. Widespread use of this style among aristocratic women in court led to its reference outside of court as "high brow."

When it comes to the military profession, in ancient and modern times alike, tradition has dictated short hair for fighting troops. This regulation allegedly started with Alexander the Great, who commanded an army that ultimately conquered the known world. As battles of those days involved sword-to-shield, hand-to-hand combat, Alexander recognized that long hair—either on scalp or beard—was a major threat, for it could be grabbed to expose and incapacitate even a heavily armed infantry soldier. He therefore instituted mandatory short hair for all his soldiers. The practice continues today, though not for any practical or logistic reason; now we associate the short, neatly kept hair of those in the military with order, discipline, and routine.

During the 18th century, using hair to send messages of political prominence reached the extreme. Members of European high society held that if lush hair advertised political health and power, then even more hair should amplify that message. To attain that end, men and women went to absurd lengths with their wigs in order to impress, an important topic we will return to later.

In the East, it was not the quantity of hair but the style that reflected one's position in the political and social realm. According to Confucian laws, society runs smoothly only when citizens adhere to their appointed places. In ancient China and Korea, hair braided in codified styles distinguished people of all societal levels and ages. For centuries, China's Manchu dynasty forced people to wear a hairstyle prescribed by their rank; the rice farmer, for example, wore a queue, a braid down the back of his head. When Sun Yat-sen, the great Chinese leader of the early 20th century, beckoned his people to overthrow the Manchu dynasty and bring the Chinese out of feudalism, he also "encouraged" them to abandon their long braided queues, an icon of the old regime. Queue-cutting became widely accepted in urban areas, but among people in the countryside, the queue was so deeply rooted in a lifestyle and cultural tradition that people strongly resisted any change, committing both murder and suicide in its defense. During this period, it seemed that many peasants valued the arrangement of their hair—or rather, the social and political values represented by their hair—over their own lives.

In the 20th century, hair continued to hold symbolic sway in the political arena. Notable is the period of the late 1960s, when the manner in which one displayed hair became an important statement of political freedom for American youth. In defiance of the older generation and its perceived buttoned-down values, adolescents to young adults—both male and female—let their hair grow. The reaction was even stronger among youth within the African-American community, who bristled under the remnants of Jim Crow laws and their spirit. On coming to America before the

Civil War, enslaved Africans had sought to adopt European hair-styles. Motivation to straighten their hair was based on the fact that Africans with more European-looking hair enjoyed greater social advantages, such as access to more favorable tasks, food, clothing, education, and opportunities for manumission. The attitude of the sixties, on the other hand, promulgated the back-to-nature spirit, but even more important, the essence of complete sociopolitical liberation. In response, many African-Americans let their hair grow out naturally without straightening, demonstrating both to themselves and the world the beauty of African hair. Yet even today, the topic of African American hair in American society is so heated that it alone could fill an entire book.

Hair also broadcasts religious messages. In Jerusalem alone, where so many different cultures travel for pilgrimages, one can see members of multiple traditions stroll alongside one another, each with their characteristic hair arrangements and covers: traditional Jewish sects with full beard, long side curls, and head covered with skull cap or fur-lined black hat; clerics from the Eastern Orthodox Church with long hair and beard; Roman Catholic pilgrims stop-ping at the Stations of the Cross wearing head scarves, wimples, coif, or cornet; and Armenian worshipers with full beard, cowl, or hood. You might also see burka-covered Muslim women, turban-wrapped Sikhs, and closely shaved Buddhist monks. In all these traditions, hair bears an essential religious meaning, and its unique presence or absence reflects the celebrant's particular covenant with his or her god.

In many societies, the act of cutting hair on one's head is consid-ered a holy act in itself. The first haircut in particular is significant in many cultures. For the Albanian mountain people, the first haircut for boys is both codified and serious. These extant Macedonian people live a life governed by the rules of the Kanun,[29] a book prescribing behavior limits and the consequences of transgression. According to the Kanun, personal honor must be protected at all costs, and any slight error in interpreting religious law—even regarding a haircut—may be construed as an insult. The Kanun states that the haircut must be performed by a male, termed the godfather. The parents "must prepare the best food they are able to provide in order to honor the godparent" and bring to the ceremony a chair for the godfather to sit, a cup of water in which the godfather must place a small silver coin, a cloth to receive the hair, and a pair of scissors or razor to shear the hair. Hair removal proceeds in a strict order: a) a lock on the forehead; b) a lock at each temple; c) a lock at the nap of the neck. After cutting the hair, the godfather taps the forehead of the godson three times with the scissors, pronouncing the phrase "health and long life." The Kanun dictates that the godfather must spend that night in the house of his godson. The next day, he brings the child and mother to his own home, where they remain for the next three to five days. At the end of this visit, the ceremony is complete. In this tradition of a boy's first haircut, we see a deep-seated cultural ritual performed with the utmost gravity, the first among many that must be properly performed.

Another "first haircut" of sorts is the ceremony of tonsure, which is a religious ceremony performed in a few different religious orders, including Roman Catholicism, the Eastern Orthodox Church, and Buddhism, in which varying portions of hair are removed from the scalp of entrants. In this ceremony, the cutting of hair signals the commitment of a novitiate to a life of devotion to God and his entry into a religious order. Three tonsures are recognized in the Christian Church: the Roman (in which the whole scalp is shorn except for a rim of hair about the temples, representing the Crown of Thorns), the Greek tonsure (in which the entire head is shorn), and the Celtic tonsure (in which all the hair on the frontal scalp is removed up to a line extending from ear to ear). In the Roman ceremony, the novitiate dresses in black cassock, with a white vestment draped over his left arm, and he holds a lit candle in his right hand. After reciting prayers, the bishop first removes five pieces of hair from the top of the novitiate's skull in the shape of a cross; he then removes hair from a circular area on the crown. As recorded by Reverend L. Bacuez, in his description of the tonsure, "In submitting his hair to the bishops' scissor, the would-be cleric gives plain token of his desire to forego wordly [sic] concerns and interests . . . a surrender of his will, the consecration of his faculties, energies, and life to the worship and service of the Church . . . [O]ne must begin [life in the clergy] with detachment from things nearest one's self."[30] While the practice was widespread in the Middle Ages, it's rarely observed in its complete form today. A modified practice of tonsure is still active in Asia: Among Buddhists, it is essential to the life of a monk, and among Hindus, it is practiced as a rite of passage—after birth, entry into school, and in periods of bereavement.

Hair plays a dominant role in human communication. It sends messages from person to person, and messages call for action. But to get the messages just right, we often need the assistance of specialists who know how to formulate and parse what we want to say. This is when the consumer must turn to the professional.

6

BARBERS AND BEAUTICIANS

—

Up until the 18th century, a barber was also a surgeon,
because hair and body care were considered indistinguishable.

I n the year 1215 C.E. at the Tenth Lateran Council, leaders of
the Roman Catholic Church deemed that it was inappropriate
for monks or any ecclesiastic to use surgical methods, ruling
that "any priest who shed blood would be officially debarred from
the higher offices of the Church."[1] With this decision, the council
reversed a decree that had been issued four hundred years earlier
by the Holy Roman Emperor Charlemagne, which stated that all
monasteries and cathedrals must have annexed hospitals staffed

by churchmen. For four centuries, monks had let blood, placed leeches, lanced boils, administered enemas, extracted teeth, and also cut, shaved, and dressed scalp and beard hair. Now the monks transferred all their tissue- and hair–cutting services to the local beard-shaving barbers, who already knew how to wield scissors and blades.[2] The new doctrine was significant because it separated care of body from care of soul.

Since the dawn of civilized man, unwell people sought the guidance of a medicine man. These spiritual caregivers took different shapes and names in different societies, but in general they served the sick by invoking and controlling the spirits of life and illness. Their holistic approach was based on the notion that health is determined by a balance between good and bad spirits, and in order to keep that balance, they employed techniques such as incantations, bloodletting, trepanning (boring holes into the skull), and hair removal to eliminate the noxious spirits. In this regimen, trimming hair was no less important than letting blood. While to the modern mind the medicine man had two jobs—to cut hair and to tend to illnesses—to the ancient mind he had one: to treat the total body. By this doctrine, treating hair and ministering to the body—the skills of barbering and surgery—were somehow equivalent.

After the Lateran Council's ruling, these new barber-surgeons formed and thrived as craftsmen throughout Europe. In recognition of their importance to English society, King Edward IV founded the first guild of barber-surgeons in 1462 and gave them, as was typical for other guilds, a monopoly over the practice of barbering and surgery in the City of London.[3] But outside of the sanctioned guild was a group of surgeons who, despite the barbers' limited charter, practiced more invasive surgeries based on their knowledge of anatomy. Though the group was small, comprising just eleven practitioners in London of 1514, it took the inflated title of Fellowship of Surgeons. When one of this group—Thomas Vicary, a university-trained surgical practitioner and author of a human anatomy book—cured King Henry VIII of a "sore leg," the king united the elite Fellowship of Surgeons with the Company of Barbers in 1540.[4] Even though the terms of this ill-conceived merger stipulated that barbers would not act as surgeons and surgeons would not act as barbers, in practice both frequently and contentiously disregarded the restraint.[5]

Despite the turf squabble, the union of barber-surgeons survived for the next two hundred years. But, with time, interests of the two groups diverged to such an extent that a schism became inevitable. This split was based on the growing realization that hair and body are separable and should be treated differently, as well as on the type of schooling and daily work routine each discipline required. The barber-surgeon, whose training consisted of an onsite apprenticeship, spent most of his day shaving, cutting hair, and performing minor surgery such as bleeding and lancing abscesses. He performed his surgical tasks oblivious of the body into which he cut. In contrast, the surgeon, whose training included university study and extensive exposure to anatomic dissection, treated complex surgical problems beyond the barber's ability, such as gunshot or lacerated wounds, ulcers, tumors, fractures of limbs or skull, and burns.[6] Because of their background, knowledge, and skillset, surgeons enjoyed an esteem the barbers lacked. They were sought out not only by people with serious health issues but also by the Royal Navy, which required trained surgeons aboard its merchant marine ships. The irreconcilable and fundamental differences between the barber-surgeons and surgeons led to their separation in 1745: The surgeons formed the Company of Surgeons (which in 1800 was renamed the Royal

College of Surgeons), and the barbers formed the Company of Barbers. Both organizations are active today.

A symbol and reminder of the barber-surgeon is the traditional barber's pole. The pole mirrors the common practice of bloodletting—releasing "bad blood"—which involved lancing an arm vessel, collecting blood in a basin, and wrapping the arm with white bandages. During this procedure, the patient gritted his teeth and gripped a pole. When not in use, the pole rested, with a clean white bandage twisted about it, in front of the shop as a sign of services rendered. Later, instead of displaying the actual pole and bandage, barbers used a painted pole that resembled the original—sometimes painted red and white (for arterial blood and bandage) and sometimes painted red, white, and blue (the blue to symbolize venous blood).[7] In the early years of barbering, the pole served as a form of governmental accreditation;[8] today, it identifies a barbershop and may even be referred to in legal documents; for example, the 2011 Pennsylvania State Barber License Law requires that "every barbershop shall provide . . . one barber pole, or a sign indicating that barbering services are performed."[9]

Up until the early 20th century, the African-American-owned barbershop was a uniquely American institution. For the freed slave it offered a venue for starting and learning a new life, for exploiting the capitalistic economy, and for enjoying the promise of freedom.[10] During the 17th and 18th centuries, although plantation owners forced the largest number of imported Africans into field work, they selected a small number of their slaves for household services, some of whom became personal servants. These "waiting men" were responsible for keeping their master looking well groomed: They polished boots, shaved beards, and cut hair. Those slaves who excelled in these skills often enjoyed exceptional privileges including better food, clothing, shelter, and education. If a master had more than one "waiting man" or a particularly efficient one, he rented him out to other wealthy men. In many cases, masters set up barbershops for their waiting men in nearby major cities, such as Richmond, Nashville, Charlotte, Baltimore, and Savannah. The shops were often upscale in service, decor, and sanitation, with ancillary services such as boot shine, cigar supply, and baths. Slave owners as well as their slave barbers profited from the revenue. Many skilled, ambitious, and entrepreneurial slave barbers became wealthy enough to buy not only the barbershop and their own freedom but also freedom for their families.[11] Successful black barbers bought their own homes, supported churches, and had their children educated. Some even bought large parcels of land and staffed them with slaves. However, there was a trade-off: Customers supporting these barbershops were whites (and often slave-owning whites), so the black barber—now a legally free shop owner—was still forced to act submissively and obsequiously. Further, the most successful shops were closed to African clients because the wealthy white clients did not want to be barbered in a shop where Africans had been tended.

As long as the white community associated barbering with slaves, black barbers dominated the trade, even in the North. Between 1860 and 1880, African Americans made up 96 percent of the barbers in Charleston, 30 percent in Philadelphia, 50 percent in Cleveland and Detroit, and 66 percent in Colorado.[12] Dominance of the African-American barbershop waned in the early 20th century as a consequence of many factors: immigration of competitive barbers from Europe, resurgence of black pride, macroeconomic stress, fall of the plantation, loss of the aristocratic white, and above all, harsh and stifling Jim Crow laws.

In the late 19th century, African-American-owned barbershops began to serve African-American clients, and the barbershop became a meeting place for black men to gather, discuss politics, share concerns, and relax. During the wait, they often sang spirituals, folk ballads, and popular songs. With time, the singing became a codified tradition; they sang *a cappella* with a rich, four-part harmony and, when giving recitals, dressed in well-groomed, barbershop-striped jackets and pants. They called themselves "barbershop quartets" and popularized such songs as "Shine On, Harvest Moon," "Sweet Adeline," and "We Are Poor Little Lambs That Have Gone Astray." The idea spread so that in the early part of the 20th century, barbershop quartets became part of most American neighborhoods, both black and white. Today, international organizations involving both men and women perform and enjoy this vocal music in concert halls far from the shops of its origin.[13]

Ben Franklin suggested that "If you teach a poor man to shave himself, and keep his razor in order, you may contribute more to the happiness of his life than in giving him a thousand guineas."[14] One can't argue with the dictum, but using a straight razor and keeping it sharp was not a skill most males of that era or earlier eras cherished. As far back as 3000 B.C.E., men and women of the ancient Egyptian Pharaonic court cropped their heads, chins, and body hairs with straight metal razors made of copper or bronze. Hardly a rapidly moving technology, the next advance in shaving blades occurred in the 17th century court of Louis XIII, where local swordsmiths developed a new type of folding straight razor made out of steel. Variations of this prototype remained popular at home and in barbershops until the early 20th century, when a resourceful American traveling salesman, King Gillette, developed, manufactured, and sold a safety razor. Because it was easy to use, encased for safety, and disposable, the Gillette razor became universally popular. Above all, it reshaped the traditional barbering experience in two ways. First, because using the safety razor was intuitive, anyone could self-shave at home: men their cheeks and chins, women their legs and underarms. Second, since men could now care for their beards at home, the barber lost the bulk of his daily customers: The fastidious dresser no longer needed a barbershop visit in his daily or weekly routine. Still, a vestige of the old shave remains in the haircut of today. Using comb, scissors, and electric clippers, the modern barber usually delivers a satisfactory trim in a manner of minutes. Now the haircut is over, but the haircut experience is not. At this point the barber puts hot suds on the nape, opens his folded straight-edge razor blade, strops it on the adjacent cowhide belt, and then shaves the neck from top to bottom in slow continuous strokes. He then wipes the remaining suds off with a warm towel and pats the shaven neck with cool witch hazel. It's only then, with the wink at tradition, that the full haircut experience is complete.

During the Middle Ages, if a lad was interested in cutting hair, he became an apprentice to a master member of the Barber Guild. After about seven years, he presented his credentials to a committee of the guild, and if the guild granted its imprimatur, the trainee was allowed to barber in the community. To find out how barbering is taught today, I visited Matt Schwalm, the director of the Barber Styling Institute in Camp Hill, Pennsylvania.

The institute is located in a cinema mall on the outskirts of town. Its central room is high ceilinged, well lit, and cream colored. Along the length of the room are two parallel rows of ten barber chairs. In each chair sits a customer, either upright or supine, attended by one student-barber, who diligently addresses the tonsorial issue of the moment. Schwalm, thirty-five years old, is an outgoing, affable, and infectiously enthusiastic hairdresser, casually dressed without uniform or lab coat. His walnut-colored hair is short on both sides and swept up into an impressive faux-Mohawk.

Schwalb explained that, until 1935, all barber training in America was conducted in an apprentice-master association where instruction was entirely up to the senior barber. After that time, the state set up standards that each trainee and shop had to meet. At the institute, applicants must have completed at least eight grades of formal schooling. Once accepted, students undergo rigorous academic and practical instruction in which state-certified instructors deliver formal lectures in a chalkboard classroom using projections and videos. Hands-on experience starts with laboratory exercises using bewigged mannequins and then progresses to the volunteer clients who fill the classroom chairs. State regulations require that each student spend 1,250 hours in formal apprenticeship before he or she is qualified to sit for the practical and written certification exams. In order to achieve competency in all aspects of barbering (which include safety, hair anatomy, physiology and pathology, infection control, shaving, haircutting, hair washing, hair coloring, permanent waving, hair straightening, and finally, familiarity with shop management and related state laws), Schwalm expects his students to master an eight-hundred-page textbook. The institute produces about twenty certified barbers per year, of which one third are women. Tuition for barber school training, inclusive of all books and materials, costs about $10,000 and takes between nine and thirteen months to complete. Although most graduates join an existing establishment, a talented and enterprising few start their own shops, but because state certification requires each barbershop to have its own essential equipment and supplies (including a mirror, a swivel barber chair, a washstand with hot and cold running water, and a hair clipper, razor, and strop), expense for the start-up barber can be a significant barrier to entry.

Although hair care for men took place in a barbershop or an equivalent site away from home, hair care for women historically took place in the privacy of their homes with the help of servants, family members, or friends. In part, the situation depended on who was permitted to touch a lady's hair; in Europe, for example, until the 17th century, the Roman Catholic Church forbade any male from handling a woman's hair—at least in public. The first commercial establishment for women's hair care opened in Paris in 1635, and although this first salon was not widely accepted, it catered largely to women who could not afford a private hairdresser. But the real launch of salons occurred in the 1870s in Paris, when a hair stylist named Marcel Grateau initiated a new way to curl hair.

Grateau started out in the hair trade as a groomer of horses in Paris. Interested in applying his skills to humans, he volunteered in his free time to help his beautician friend in one of the few salons in the city. By age twenty, he had learned enough about women's hair to open his own operation in the Montmartre district, at that time an artistic and less affluent Parisian neighborhood. A creative and venturesome person, he experimented with different methods for waving hair and found that a combination of curling irons, pressure, and heat gave stable hair patterns. By this approach, he could place natural-appearing, undulating waves—which came to be called "Marcel waves"—into hair of any length. So attractive was this style that women in Paris and beyond outbid each other for appointments with him.[15] His successes not only attracted a wide clientele, but they solidified and legitimized the concept of an independent, home-away salon for women's hair care. Today, salons are part of the life of the modern woman, and the demand is served by more than one hundred thousand shops in the United States alone.

But in order to practice the trade, a conscientious hair stylist has got to know what hair is: how it's made, how it frays, how it curls, and how it forms locks.

THE HAIR-HANG ACT

⌒

A lock of ten thousand hairs is strong enough to lift more than one adult person.

A thin, flat-chested woman dressed in a simple, sequined, loose-fitting leotard stands encircled by a gaggle of fussy attendants. She stares distantly and impassively beyond the audience. A short, muscular male knots her long, straight, black hair and then braids it into an equally thick rope, which is suspended from rafters high above the stage. The attendants withdraw and the woman raises her arms winglike; the rope straightens, her hair lifts, and she slowly rises. Throughout the ascent, she locks her head and holds her gaze. At the apogee, she pirouettes with pointed toes and chest-crossed arms. As she unspins, she opens her arms, flashes a simper, throws a tenuous kiss, and descends slowly to the thrill of the circus crowd. The audience cheers, amazed by the fact that this woman can be lifted by her hair.

In the laboratory, a single healthy human scalp hair can lift about a quarter pound without breaking, so the shaft itself has considerable tensile strength. The other end of this remarkable act depends on anchorage: After all, if we picked the performer up by her hairs and the hairs fell out at the root, she would drop, her hairs would stay in the rafters, her trainer would sue, and the audience would want their money back. Scientists have found that it takes about a fifth of a pound of force to pull out one growing scalp hair shaft from the deep skin. If the knot of hair holding this acrobat consisted of only ten thousand hairs (and it probably contained many more), it could lift about fifteen hundred pounds. Of course, part of the real wow factor for a successful "hair-hang" is due to the incredible strength and flexibility of the neck bones and joints, but it would be impossible without the unique physical properties of hair.

A hair shaft is constructed something like the trunk of a tree. They are both built to withstand extreme physical stress. Each is solid and cylindrical in shape. Each is made of spindle-shaped cells and threadlike molecules. Each is wrapped on the outside by a layer, called "cuticle" in the hair and "bark" in the tree.

It is there, though, that the parallel between a tree trunk and hair shaft ends. Whereas the tree trunk is made of cells and structural materials found in plants, the hair follicle is composed of cells and molecules found only in higher animals. The cells making up the tree trunk are living; in contrast, the cells making up the hair shaft are dead. The way the two cylinders grow is also fundamentally different. A tree trunk expands by means of annual growth rings arising from cells in the bark that proliferate upward and outward. Hair shaft elongation, meanwhile, occurs when cells in the deep hair follicle divide and add to the shaft base, pushing the growing hair fiber upward.

The hair shaft forms from epithelial cells alone; it has no blood vessels or nerves: If cut, it does not bleed; if bent, it does not hurt. The shaft starts growing within the deep hair follicle where the most actively dividing cells reside. The cells at its base are cuboidal in shape but as they move up the shaft, they stretch: Their shape becomes cylindrical and then threadlike. As these cells mature, they attach to one another and fill with threadlike proteins called keratins. When completely mature, the hair shaft is a dry, fossilized thread, with no living cells but possessing a formidably strong structure, just as the hair-hang act illustrates.

The threadlike proteins filling the cells, the keratins, serve like bridge suspensions extending from one cell wall to another. While the keratin filaments attach to one another and to the cell wall, they are also embedded and locked into a surrounding cytoplasmic glue.[1] How and what keratins fill the cell determines the shape of the shaft cell and in turn the shape of the shaft itself. First of all, keratins do not always pack the cell evenly. In a curling hair, for example, keratin packing of cells on the inside of the bend is different from keratin packing of cells on the outside of the bend. And how the keratins pack influences the type of hair curl.[2] Second, each shaft is made of multiple different kinds of keratin proteins. In fact, the term "keratin" refers to a large family of proteins, each with a similar shape with loose, floppy tops and bottoms. Although the central portion of all keratins shows a very similar chemical makeup, the end portions are unique to each keratin type. Scientists have identified twenty-four different keratin proteins in human hair. Though they do not yet know why so many are needed for such a simple-looking structure, they believe that each keratin type plays a unique role in hair shaft formation, shape, and texture. Because keratins are not interchangeable, deficiency of any one keratin can be a major problem. For example, a child born with a genetic inability to make hair keratin type hHb6 grows hair—but the child's hair has abnormally shaped shafts. The defect has been named *monilethrix* (for *monile* meaning "necklace" and *thrix* meaning "hair") because the deficient hair shaft looks like a pearl necklace with regions of hills and dales. These shafts are extremely brittle, so that even mild trauma such as combing can break them at the point of thinning—in the valleys. For this reason, monilethrix hairs break soon after they reach the skin surface, leaving the patient with a hair-scant, if not entirely hairless, scalp. While we know the defective gene, the missing protein, and where it is expressed in the hair shaft, we do not yet understand how this particular keratin interacts with the community of keratins to maintain hair shaft integrity, how its absence leads to disease, and, most frustrating of all, how to repair the defect.

Genetic conditions aside, a healthy hair is one of the longest-lasting structures in the body, behind bone and tooth. When hair is buried in a dry environment, it can last for tens of thousands of years. But when buried in a warm, moist soil, the hair shaft will fall apart within weeks or even days. This is mostly due to the fact that the shaft is made of protein; from 85 to 99 percent of a dry hair shaft is protein. Considering that the protein content of hamburger meat or a well-marbled steak ranges from 17 to 22 percent, these common foods have nothing over the hair shaft—if you could eat it. Actually, some organisms can and do. The trenchermen in this case are a variety of bacteria and fungi found in moist soil, which use unique enzymes, appropriately called keratinases, to digest the keratins. These bugs cleave the highly cross-linked keratins into bite-sized portions and then gorge on the resultant banquet. Such organisms may also feast on human hair. In the disease ringworm, for example, fungi invade scalp hair. The fungus attaches to the hair shaft, insinuates itself into it, and promptly digests it, either outside-in or inside-out, causing the hair to thin, break off, and leave patchy, hairless spaces on the scalp. Among school children, ringworm can spread like wildfire through an entire unsuspecting grammar school class. Happily, today we have drugs that kill such fungi, thus preventing further hair shaft destruction and allowing new shaft formation.

Besides these fungi, most other organisms do not have the ability to digest keratins. One example is a 13,000-year-old ground sloth that was found with well-preserved hairs in its gut.[3] Most modern cat owners know hairballs can be an issue for their feline friends, but hairballs can also be a problem in the human gastrointestinal tract. In one recently reported case, a fourteen-year-old girl came to the hospital with severe stomach cramps. Emergency surgeons found she had a six-inch-diameter hairball in her stomach and diagnosed her conditions as "Rapunzel syndrome," an intestinal complication arising after humans ingest hair.[4] (The surgeons who named this syndrome thought that the hairball with its strands trailing in the intestine looked something like the flowing hair of the eponymous storybook character.) The girl did well after her surgeon removed the hair obstruction, but typical of her case, as well as others, is that she suffered from a psychiatric disorder driving her to pull out and eat her own hair. Rapunzel's syndrome and its resulting complications illustrate two properties of hair: First, it is a tough material not readily broken down in the intestine, and second, the ingested hairs that end up in the cramped, warm, and wet environment of the gut can snowball into a large, tightly bound, obstructive mass.

When hair is wet, warm, and compressed, it can form a tightly entangled collection of fibers. In other words, it felts. Hair is able to felt because its surface is covered by a cuticle, a layer of cells that encircles the shaft. The cuticle and the properties it imposes on the hair are unique to hair; it is not present on silk, cotton, flax, hemp, or any other natural fiber.[5] Because cuticle cells stick up a bit, cuticle cells of one shaft are able to hook onto cuticle cells of an adjacent shaft. You can observe an important feature of the hair cuticle by pinching a lock of hair with your thumb and forefinger and sliding your clamped fingers up and down. On the way up (away from your scalp), the trip is smooth, while on the way down (toward your scalp), you should feel some resistance. The resistance is due to the fact that cuticle cells lie like tiles of a roof: On the roof surface, the tiles point toward the rooftop and on the hair shaft surface the cuticle cells point toward the skin surface. Because the cuticle cells project away from the shaft tip, they give to the outward-growing shaft the ability to scoop up and carry to the skin surface any loose, unwanted material from the deep hair canal, such as dust particles, shed cells, and sebaceous oils. They also impose a significant deterrent, if not a near-complete barrier, to insects crawling on hair shafts from the tip toward the skin surface.

Cuticle orientation is the same on all hairs of your body and all hairs of other mammals except for one: the porcupine quill. The porcupine's quill is a modified rigid, sharp-tipped, enormous hair arising on the back skin of a porcupine. Depending on the species, quills may be clustered in one region or interspersed diffusely amongst other fur hairs. When the animal is alarmed, its quill follicle muscle pulls the quill upright. The quill cuticle points outward, like an arrowhead, toward the tip (unlike your own hairs). The reversed orientation has two significant consequences. First, the quill cannot hold onto its follicle base; it is very loosely moored.

Second, when the quill punctures any tissue, it acts like the barb on a fishing hook and is extremely difficult to extract; moreover, small movements will shimmy the quill deeper and deeper into tissues. Because of their cuticle cell orientation, these hairs are real killers.[6]

The ratchetlike ladder of the cuticle gives the shaft its strong anchoring properties. Like the moveable hinges of an airplane wing, cuticle cells flap open when they are in a humid or wet environment. Cuticle cells of the shaft are present in this open configuration in the humid, deep follicle, but here an amazing interaction takes place. Just outside of the deep hair shaft the enveloping layer of the follicle wall also contains its own cuticle, identical to the cuticle of the hair shaft—but pointing in the other direction, away from the skin surface. In this way, when the flared cuticle of the lower hair shaft opens, it hooks onto the flared cuticle of the follicle wall. What happens to the cuticle and hair shaft in the deep follicle is similar to what happens to it in the felting process.

Folk legend has it that felting was inadvertently discovered by St. Clement, the fourth bishop of Rome and the patron saint of hatters. Clement was apparently a fellow with rather tender feet. The legend goes that while fleeing a persecuting mob, he stuffed his shoes with sheep wool. Upon reaching safety, he removed his shoes to find that the wool was no longer a loose fluff, but a tight, firm cloth. His warm, moist feet had pounded the loose wool as he bounded away from his pursuers, forcing the wool fibers to intertwine and the cuticle cells to open and interlock—in other words, to felt. The industrial process of felting uses the same steps: collect wool, wet it, heat it, and pound it.

Compared to other fabrics, which require weaving, felt-making is easy. In the felt cloth industry, the choice starting material is merino sheep wool, which consists of very fine curled and cuticle-prominent fibers. The felt worker first washes the wool, then combs it into a sheet of loosely packed, aligned fibers called a batt. Next, she piles batt layers perpendicularly on top of each other until she forms the desired thickness. For a hat, she would need just one or two batt layers, while for a blanket or rug, she would use many more. The actual felting process involves placing the layered batts into warm, soapy water and then rolling, kneading, and pounding them. The batt is considered felted once it has formed a solid, dense mass; at this point the wool fibers are so tightly enmeshed that extraction of individual fibers is virtually impossible.

Like the fiber from which it is made, felt is tough and its applications have been impressively broad. Once completely formed, felt cloth reflects the properties of the hair cortex. It is lightweight and resistant to high pressures, intense vibration, and excessive stretching. Because it is a poor conductor of heat and electricity, it is resistant to high temperatures, electrical charge, and fire. Felt absorbs its weight in water without becoming wet; moreover, when it takes up water, it gives up heat. As there are no loose fibers, felt does not ravel, fray, or shrink. Felt can be made so hard, it can be carved, drilled, and even turned on a lathe. Because other materials were not available during World War II, felt use was taken to the extreme; it was used for airplane bulkhead insulation, weatherstripping, gas mask air filters, boots, canteen cover linings, caps, coats, ski boots, radio chassis gaskets, periscope cases, truck wheel cylinder covers, car door bumpers, artificial feet and hands, tourniquet pads, polishing bobs, wheels, and more.

Though physical evidence of felt extends only as far back as the Neolithic period, around 6500 B.C.E., archeologists believe humans felted wool well before they wove it. The first use may have been among the nomadic people of Central Asia (including Turkey, Afghanistan, Iran, Mongolia, and Turkestan), who worked felt into hats and huts, shoes and saddles, coats and carpets. With felt so important to their everyday life, the ancient Chinese (400 B.C.E.) referred to the country of these nomadic people as the "the land of felt."[7] It is thought these were the people who transferred the skills of felting to Western Europeans more than thirty-five hundred years ago. The Europeans had many uses for felt, but perhaps the most common was felt hats. Sailors and soldiers of ancient Greece wore a brimless felt hat, the pileus. Homer tells us that even the wily Odysseus wore a felt hat under his helmet. In Rome, it was the custom for a slave to celebrate his freedom by shaving his head and replacing the long hair of servitude with a felt cap, so the cap became a badge of liberty. The Persian king Xerxes and his soldiers wore felt hats into battle: The soldiers' hats fit tightly over their heads while the king's hat was pointed like a cock's comb. Even today, there is something about felt hats that resonates: fedoras, homburgs, and berets among Europeans, fezzes in the Middle East, and the characteristic bowler hats among the Quechua and Aymara peoples of South America.

While most felt is made from sheep's wool, felt can also be made from the underfur of other animals such as rabbit, muskrat, otter, cat, or dog. In fact, any hair with a normal cuticle will work. One doesn't usually think of felting human hair because human hair doesn't felt very well, but human hair can indeed felt, as seen with the tight hairball of Rapunzel's syndrome or with dreadlocks. Hair stylists can generally make locks using any hair from any human group by repeating the steps of felt making: wetting the hair, heating it, and pressing it into shape. But as certain hair types are easier to felt than others, the stylist must be aware of the different hairs people grow and how hairs can be manipulated. For the stylist, it's all about understanding hair itself to achieve the desired look.

8

COMB, SCISSORS, CURLER, DYE

—

Permanent curling, straightening, coloring, or bleaching requires destruction and reconstruction of the hair fiber.

Early 20th-century physical anthropologists contended that humans could be classified into "races" based on broad generalizations regarding skin color and hair character. For them, hair shape—be it straight, wavy, or tightly curled—dictated geographic origin: long, straight, black hair for Asians; tightly curled or kinky hair for sub-Saharan Africans; and wavy hair for Indo-Europeans.

The early physical anthropologists were right in that there are important hair differences between ethnic groups, but, today, we recognize that hair shape alone does not necessarily foretell geography, ethnicity, or family history. One reason is that the global human community has interbred for a long time and unmixed human populations are rare, if they exist at all. Consider how the large number of "pure" Europeans walking around today acquired Neanderthal genes in their hair follicles.[1] Another reason is that there is considerable overlap between hair types within so-called "racial" groups. In a traditional European population, there are people with predominately straight and others with predominately kinky-curled hair. Within traditional African populations, there are people with straight hair. A similar broad range of hairs is found among Asians. Japanese industrial scientist Dr. Shinobu Nagase and colleagues found that 53 percent of Japanese women have straight hair and 47 percent have some curved hair, varying from slightly wavy to frizzy.[2,3] Moreover, in all ethnic groups, body hair is curled. So one isolated hair cannot tell us much about the origins of the grower.

Because of the extensive overlap in hair shaft types, some researchers have suggested that we characterize hair shafts not by the presumed "racial" origin of the grower, but by the curvature of the shafts.[4] Professor Gildas Loussouarn and colleagues in Paris have conducted studies that suggest human hairs can be classified into eight different levels of curve and that all eight groups can be found in all populations of the world.[5] The point is that in assessing how to treat hair—be it in a barbershop, hair salon, or medical clinical—the hair type is paramount, not the social, political, or geographic origin of the person who grew it.[6]

The challenge to styling different kinds of hairs starts right away, in combing. Although untangling is essential to good hair care, excessive combing of any kind of hair will, in time, injure the shaft surface and strip the cuticle.[7] A hair shaft without its cuticle is like a maki-sushi without its nori cover: Both lose their shape as their fundamentals bulge out of place. Without a cuticle, the threadlike cells of the hair shaft flare, giving shagginess to its end, generating what we call "split ends." Unfortunately, because it is made of dead cells, a shaft is unable to repair itself; split hairs are permanent.[8]

Resistance to combing is directly related to the degree of curliness. Combing curled hair inevitably leads to a battle between the comber and the incorrigible lock because combing involves not only untwisting the curl but also attempting to untie it, since curly hairs tend to intertwine and knot. This battle scene is played out when mother tries to comb the long, curly locks of her screaming daughter before the school bus arrives.

People with long, tightly curled hair learn that combing is a lot easier if their hair is straightened or well oiled. Although shampoos are essential for good hair and scalp health, soaps tend to remove natural oils and, in so doing, increase hair stickiness, which makes the combing job even harder. In order to put back what shampoos take out, cosmetic manufacturers provide products that coat hair shafts and reduce hair-to-hair and hair-to-comb interactions. These materials may be incorporated into shampoos or provided separately. Conditioners and creme rinses contain long pole-shaped molecules, one end of which will attach to the hair shaft and the other end of which will impart to the shaft surface a positive charge.[9] Since all hairs coated by the product now have a positive charge and because positives repel positives, these hairs will be less likely to knot and more likely to fall straight. For very tightly curled hair, heavier, oily materials—such as pomades (mineral oil, lanolin, and petrolatum), oils, and waxes—may be necessary to facilitate combing.

The very first hairs to appear on the earliest mammals were probably straight because designing and growing straight hair requires less complex molecular machinery. Today, virtually all modern mammals are covered with both straight and curled hairs. Curled hairs offer more efficient skin surface protection because they cover a greater area of skin per unit of hair length, assuring a better shield and insulation. Stiff, straight, thick hairs that do not intertwine with one another do not cover as much skin as densely curled, intertwining thin hairs.[10]

Among the features of humanness is passion for what we do not have. Regarding hair, that often translates into straightening our curled hair or curling our straight hair; either way, people go to great lengths to alter the lay of their shafts. In order to understand how curls can be produced, it is first important to think back to the structure of the hair shaft itself in a little more detail. The hair shaft is made of a fibrous core surrounded by a wrap-around outer layer of cuticle cells. Cells making up these layers are filled with thread-shaped proteins called keratins and the keratins in turn sit in a gummy glue rich in sulfur groups, like cat-o'-nine tails growing in a mephitic muddy swamp. The keratin proteins are bound to one another and to the surrounding materials by means of two types of chemical connections, weak and strong attachments. The weak attachments are referred to as hydrogen bonds. By wetting hair, you break the weak hydrogen bonds and loosen the shaft structure: Hair relaxes when it is in water or exposed to high humidity. These bonds give hair the ability to take up lots of water (in fact, a hair shaft will take up its weight in water), and a water-soaked hair shaft is very stretchable. In the curling process, the beautician wets hair to open the weak hydrogen bonds and then re-forms them in the shape of the curler. This is essentially how Marcel Grateau achieved his famous waves in Paris in the 1870s using his curling iron. The curling clamp consists of a metal central prong and an outer cuff. Marcel heated the curling iron and then clamped a tress of moist hair between the prong and cuff. The moisture and heat broke the structural hair hydrogen bonds, but then, as the hair dried and cooled, the hydrogen bonds re-formed to give the clamped shafts a circular shape. (The same principle can be applied to hair-straightening, but for straightening the hot prong and cuff are flat.) The trade-off for this simple and relatively safe procedure is that the new shape is water-sensitive. If the newly curled hair is exposed to water or high humidity, the weak hydrogen bonds break again and the hair slips back to what the shaft looked like at the start. Using these hydrogen bonds to mold hair is thus easy, quick, and safe—but hardly long-lasting.

A second way of straightening or curling hair is by breaking and remaking the strong sulfur bonds that bind keratins to each other. Because these bonds are very stable, once you break and re-form them, the changes are permanent; water or shampooing will not bring back the original hair shape. The strong sulfur bonds holding keratins together can be broken by sulfur-rich chemicals—"relaxers"—which are supplied in a hair permanent kit. When the breaking chemicals are washed out with a weak acid (such as vinegar-smelling acetic acid), the strong bonds re-form and the hair takes on the shape of the curler. Although this process delivers a cosmetically desirable shape, it also permanently alters the physical properties of hair, leaving it less pliable, and more brittle. And it must be noted: The recipe must be followed meticulously, because exposure to too much relaxer will turn any hair shaft—thick or thin, curled or straight—into mush.

Affecting hair curl is one major tool for those seeking to change their look, but so is hair color. Although we didn't dwell on it in chapter 5, colors make up an inseparable part of the messages hair sends, and people around the globe spend more than $10 billion each year on hair dyeing.[11]

Hair hues all convey specific impressions and prejudices. First of all, hair color betrays biological age: Light colors indicate infancy, while strong, full colors signify youth, and gray or white hair age.[12] But there are other, more nuanced connotations. In the tradition of Western fairy tales, wicked witches either have long black or gray hair while the damsel-in-distress invariably has long, flowing, blond hair. (Admittedly, Snow White is a refreshing exception.) Blond hair has been important for adult European women as far back as ancient Rome because, to them, yellow hair evokes luminosity of heavenly light, reflections of gold, a state of purity, and an aura of youth. In contrast, red hair has historically had negative connotations. For the churchgoer during the Middle Ages, red hair designated a person who was *prima facie* evil. According to scholars of the time, Judas Iscariot, who betrayed Jesus, had red hair—the same color as the Devil himself. Red-tressed females were believed to have fiery tempers and unusually aggressive sexual appetites, while red-headed males were considered weak and sexually distasteful.

Color comes to the hair shaft from a group of unique cells that rest at the base of the hair follicle, just above the dermal papilla. These cells manufacture a deep brown pigment called melanin and are called melanocytes. These cells have numerous fine, treelike branches that reach out and touch the surface of the hair shaft cell. Upon sensing the melanocyte, the shaft cell bites off a piece of the melanocyte branch tip and gets a mouthful of melanin. In this way, the melanin incorporates into the hair shaft cell cytoplasm and the shaft becomes colored from base to tip. Hair shaft cells pick up melanin as long as the hair follicle remains in the anagen phase, that is, as long as the hair shaft is growing. The difference between heavily pigmented and lightly pigmented hair shafts is due to the number and shape of the melanin packets transferred to the shaft cells. Deep black hair contains numerous football-shaped melanin packets that sit individually. Lightly pigmented hair has far fewer melanin packets, which are clumped together and round in shape.

When we talk about hair color, we spend a lot of time discussing its loss—or what Shakespeare called "the ashes of his youth" in his seventy-third sonnet. This is, of course, gray hair. Dermatologists generalize that 50 percent of the North American population has graying of 50 percent of the scalp by the age of fifty. However, there are exceptions to the rule. Some families show the onset of gray hair in the midtwenties or earlier, while others show minimal graying even in the ninth decade. There are also certain trends that can be found between ethnic groups: Among Caucasians, graying occurs in the midthirties, among Asians in the late thirties, and Africans in the midforties.

The onset of gray hair occurs in a pattern, though that pattern can differ from person to person. In many people, hair at the side of the head turns gray first, followed by the top of the head, then the beard and then body hair. In others, gray hair forms first on the top of the head, while some men find that their beards are the first to go gray. In the earliest stages of graying, individual hairs may show a pigment stutter where part of the shaft is gray and other parts are normally colored. Eventually, the whole shaft becomes gray because very little pigment is deposited in the hair shaft cells. Although scientists around the world are studying the mechanisms of hair shaft pigmentation and hair graying, we do not yet have a clear understanding how this occurs and how to treat it.

Both to counteract graying and to make a fashion statement, men and women alike have been coloring their hair for thousands of years. Early hair dyes included minerals (such as lead, silver, iron, mercury, and nickel salts), plant derivatives (such as henna, tannin, chamomile, sage, indigo, woad, berry, and walnut extract), and carbonized plant and animal materials to make kohl (a black powder suspended in a wax or rosewater base). Most of these early colorants merely painted the surface of the hair shaft, so they lasted only up to the first wash.

With the success of the chemical industries in the late 19th century, the opportunities for creative hair coloring opened. Peroxides, which could remove natural pigments by oxidation, hit the market, as did various chemicals capable of adding new pigments. Those chemicals colored hair permanently by penetrating the shaft surface.

The most common procedure for permanently dyeing hair involves three steps.[13] First, the natural hair color must be stripped. To do this, an oxidizing compound (such as hydrogen peroxide with an alkali, like ammonia) is added to the hair. Together, these compounds relax the cuticle, make the shaft surface porous, and break up the melanin molecule. By reducing or destroying melanin, the shaft becomes blond to white. For those seeking the bleached-blond look, the process ends here. For those who want color, the dyeing process requires a second step in which a mixture of dyes is applied to the now-porous shaft. The dye molecules diffuse through the chemically altered and flared-open cuticle into the substance of the shaft. There, the dyes bind to one another and to the surrounding keratin. The chemical process is rigidly defined: Amount of dye and the application time must be perfectly balanced in order to achieve the desired result. To finish the dye job, the hair must be washed and dried in order to return hair pH to neutral, shrink the cortex, and close the cuticle. The dye is now locked in both shaft and cuticle.[14]

The natural hair shaft is made to endure, but dyeing—like hair curling or straightening—alters it forever. The permanent coloring process causes permanent damage to the shaft; it is now weakened, brittle, and porous. Although industrial scientists are striving to reduce the shaft damage inherent in this process, they recognize that the ideal solution would be to change hair color by stimulating or inhibiting the pigment cells of the normal hair follicle. This would entail some sort of prodding of the follicle melanocytes to distribute more or less melanin to growing shaft cells in order to get the desired hue.

It's an exciting future but, at present, we need a lot more insight into the normal mechanism of hair shaft formation and pigmentation before this idea becomes a reality. As a result, today, for the hair shaft shape or color changes we desire, we are restricted to harsh but effective chemical methods. However, a person either unwilling or unable to undergo hair-damaging treatments does have another choice: a wig.

9

THE ULTIMATE ARTIFICE

———

Some of the highest quality and least expensive hair used for wigs today comes from Hindu temples in the Andhra Pradesh region of India, where it is estimated that a quarter of the fifty thousand daily visitors sacrifice their hair, resulting in more than five hundred tons of hair that is sold to wig merchants annually.

The word "wig" is derived from the word "periwig," which is what the English thought they heard when the French introduced them to their word: *perruque*. In the 17th and 18th centuries, "periwig" referred specifically to a wig worn by men, composed of white, curled human or animal hair of variable length and style. Today, polite society most often softens references to wigs with such euphemisms as "hair covering" or "hairpiece," eschewing the historic terms "toupee" and "postiche."

Since earliest times, humans have used hair-mimicking head covers for societal and political reasons. As recorded in ancient texts, sculptures, and paintings, wig use was widespread in ancient Egypt, especially in the life of the royals and their court. It was common for both men and women of the higher classes to shave their heads and then wear full wigs made of human hair or date palm fibers. Not only did wigs decorate the top of the head, but they also embellished the pharaonic chin. Men, and occasionally women, wore long, cylindrical chin wigs at court as a mark of authority; these chin-wigs varied in presentation from straight to elegantly braided. Wig-wearing extended to the high societies of ancient Greece and Rome. So important were these wigs to social life that some noble Roman women kept blond household slaves in order to assure an ample supply of flaxen hair for their own hairpieces.

Wig use waned during the Middle Ages and didn't return until 1624, when Louis XIII covered his prematurely balding scalp with a long, dark, wavy-locked hairpiece. Said to be the first wig in any royal court since ancient Egyptian times, the hairpiece kicked off a new fashion that persisted for almost two hundred years, ending with the French Revolution, when royal heads and wigs were separated from royal bodies. In that pre-revolutionary society, wigs broadcasted aristocracy and power. By the end of Louis XIII's reign in 1643, wigs were accepted as required dress for nobles all over Europe and, in order to supply those wigs, the first wig guild was founded in France in 1665.

Wigs were popular in all social classes, though people at the top of the social scale wore the biggest. These massive wigs not only covered the head but also the back and shoulders. In the extreme, an attractive wig would have incorporated into it model ships, bird cages, and flags. These massive wigs were difficult to take care of, as their size prevented regular washing and the powder used to dust them—meant to add a pale patina and made of flour and starch—fed a whole host of bacteria residing on the sweaty scalp.

The wig fashions of England in the 17th and 18th centuries paralleled those of the French court. One style, the macaroni, is particularly notable. In the 1760s, upper-class young men who had taken the Grand Tour of Europe often returned home from Italy with a craving for macaroni pasta—a food new to the English of that time—and a novel hairstyle: a large white wig, very high in the front with a ribbon down the back. These dandies (essentially the predecessors to the metrosexual, with their fastidious eating, affected speech, and painstaking fashion choices) became known as "macaronis." Reference to this fashion appears in the "Yankee Doodle" song of American Revolutionary tradition where a fellow comes to town and all he need do is "put a feather in his cap" in order to become "macaroni."

Today, there are few people in the world who know more about wigmaking than Richard Mawbey. On a cool and clear autumn day in 2012, I visited him at his London workplace, a white stucco, two-storied building—a converted pub, I later learned—in a workingman's neighborhood, on a street lined by low apartment buildings. There's a small, unassuming sign on the door that hints at what happens inside: "Wig Specialties, Ltd."

Mawbey's four-decade-long career has spanned movies, television, and theater, including both Broadway and the West End. He has been the personal wigmaker for Sir Sean Connery, Kylie Minogue, and Dame Edna Everage, and he has made wigs for clients as varied as Albert Finney, Jessica Lange, Dame Judi Dench,

Leona Lewis, Susan Sarandon, and Madonna. For Mawbey, his formal education ended at the age of seventeen, when he left school to work in a beauty parlor. There he quickly excelled to become the best and most sought-after beautician in the shop. Three years later, Danny La Rue, a highly acclaimed drag actor in London, hired him as personal assistant and hair care specialist. On the first day of work, La Rue assigned Mawbey the care of more than forty wigs, which meant cleaning, repairing, and eventually remaking hairpieces. The day-to-day demand for quality wigs as well as the exposure to excellent wig makers constituted his education in wig design and manufacture. After ten years under La Rue's tutelage, Mawbey grabbed the opportunity to work on the 1986 Broadway production of *La Cage aux Folles*, a musical requiring the manufacture and maintenance of 125 wigs. After the show, Mawbey started his own firm in London. Since then, he has worked on *Evita* and *Priscilla, Queen of the Desert* on Broadway, *Frost/Nixon*, *Hairspray*, and *Legally Blonde* in London, and on movies including *Titanic, Star Wars, The Mask of Zorro*, and *The Pianist*. He also did Richard Harris's hair for the character Dumbledore in the Harry Potter movies. He freelances internationally on theater, film, and television projects and still maintains a host of private clients.

Mawbey says that the foremost step in wigmaking starts with the question: Why does this person need a wig? There are four main reasons for the wig requests that come through his door: illness (the goal being to give the appearance of health or hide a hair disorder); religion (the need to cover hair because tradition commands it); social pressure (the desire to comply with a style or convention); and theater (requiring a certain look to suit a character). Each reason results in a different process.

For the group of clients wanting to conceal a health problem or to cope with hair loss (as in the wake of chemotherapy), the wigmaker must use all of his tricks to design a head cover indistinguishable from normal hair. In other words, the main objective for this kind of wig is for the client to appear just as he or she did before the hair loss. It's helpful if the wigmaker can meet the client before she loses her hair—say, before initiating chemotherapy—in order to record optimal hair length, curl, color, and style. In fact, some patients anticipating chemotherapy may have the option of supplying their own hair for a wig, if the hair is strong enough and hasn't been permanently curled, straightened, or dyed.

People seeking wigs for religious reasons have different end goals, and their wigs can look more like wigs. In the United States, the largest use of wigs for religious purposes is among Orthodox Jewish women. In this religious tradition, a woman shows her natural hair only to her husband and immediate family, so, at the time of her marriage, she begins covering her hair. Although there are different forms of acceptable head hair covers (including scarfs, caps, and hats), a wig—called a *sheitel*, the Yiddish word for wig—is the convention. The wigmaker fashions the most common *sheitel* from uniformly brown or brunette hair, often with heavy bangs to obscure the hairline. If made of natural hair, commercially manufactured *sheitels* must bear certification that the hair used is kosher, which means it did not arise from non-kosher animals or from humans making an idolatrous sacrifice. These wigs can be particularly challenging to make, as the wig designer must strike a balance between a wig that is austere enough to be acceptable to the community and yet attractive enough to the customer. In this tradition wigs must not be too realistic, for if they are, others in the community will question if the head-cover convention has been respected.[1]

Still other clients choose to wear wigs for purely cosmetic reasons. Today, wigs used for style are made for a mostly female market and a wig may be very convenient when hair care is a time-consuming and expensive daily chore. The main advantage of wigs is that on a so-called "bad hair" day, a woman can choose from her collection of wigs and, without much fuss, put on her hair and start off the day. Because African hair often demands more beauty care, wigs are very popular within the African-American female community where it is not uncommon for an individual to have multiple wigs and spend hundreds of dollars per month for their purchase and upkeep. In most cases, wigs intended for fashion and style require fastidious design and workmanship to reproduce the natural look.

The bulk of Mawbey's business, though, comes from his commercial work in film, television, and theater. Just as the best wigs are custom-designed, woven, and fitted for one individual, so it is for each character in a story, play, or musical. In dramatic roles, the wig makes the character: David Suchet becomes *Hercule Poirot*, the Belgian detective created by Agatha Christie, when he applies a heavily waxed, pointed moustache. Sean Connery becomes James Bond when he augments his normally bald scalp with a lush, well-groomed hairpiece.

First and foremost, the wigmaker must have fibers. A wig can be made of any kind of hair or fiber—be it human, animal, plant, or synthetic—just as long as it is strong and long enough to tie. For a natural look, though, pure human hair is the most desirable.[2] There are many variations among kinds of human hair. Asian hair is the strongest, but it is also the hardest to work with because it is thick, straight, and black. In contrast, African hair is soft and silky and, as the most fragile kind of hair, the least practical for most kinds of wigmaking.

The first challenge is to find and collect the right kind of human hair for the planned wig. Most natural hair in the current market comes from South America and Asia. In Peru, hair merchants drive to a village, set up tables in the central plaza, and buy hair from the women who line up—the vast majority of whom are very poor and rely upon these visits as a source of income. In India, women donate their hair as a votive offering to Venkateswara, an incarnation of Vishnu who has the power to absolve sins. It is estimated that a quarter of the fifty thousand pilgrims who visit the temples daily in the Andhra Pradesh region donate their hair. The temple then sells the hair—more than one ton per day—to merchants. This hair is the least expensive of the high-quality wig hair on the market today.[3]

In preparation for cutting, the donor arranges her hair into multiple ponytails, binding each with several rubber bands. Once cut, the ponytails are called hanks. In the cutting process, it is critical that the individual hair shafts be kept in their normal base-to-tip orientation so the wigmaker can be confident of the shaft cuticle direction. If hairs are haphazardly placed in a wig with no concern for cuticle direction, the hairs will not only fall abnormally, they will also stick and knot to one another in the fashion of felt.

Merchant collectors sell the hair hanks to wholesalers, or hair processors, who prepare the hair for wigmakers. The first step in the preparation is cleaning, an important step because in most cases hanks come from impoverished people who live under less than hygienic conditions. The hanks are gently laundered in warm, soapy water and disinfected with chemicals or heat to remove dirt, grease, bacteria, fungi, and insects. The hair is then rinsed copiously with water and oven-dried.

Next, the wholesaler sorts the hanks into hair and color types. The value of hair in the primary market varies with hair quality, length, and type. The best hair for wigs is "virginal"—hair that has never been dyed, permed, or processed in any way, so that the shaft and cuticle are intact. Hair from long-haired, blond women of Northern or Eastern European descent is the most expensive because it is the most versatile; it is the easiest to tie into a wig net, to curl, and to straighten and, if necessary, to dye in order to match the hair color of the wearer. The price ranges from the blonds and reds of Eastern Europe (costing $100 or more for a two-foot hank) to the straight, black Peruvian or Indian hair (costing $20 per hank).

Although European hair may be optimal for the wigmaker (at least for the European market), since there's not enough to go around, the available hair is supplemented by Asian hair. Because heavily pigmented Asian hair may not always suit lightly pigmented Europeans, the wholesaler will bleach and dye the hair before he delivers it to the wigmaker, even though the process of dyeing irreversibly damages the cuticle and cortex, rendering shaft less elastic, more brittle, and consequently of lesser quality.

To get the right presentation, it is not unusual for wigmakers to blend hairs from various sources. In any one hairpiece, strands may arise from two or more human individuals or even from different animals such as yak, horse, and sheep. For example, even though he has contact with hair merchants all over the world, Mawbey cannot get enough long gray or pure white virgin human hair for his white, gray, or streaked wigs. To satisfy this need, he uses the silky, straight, pure white belly hair of the yak.

Animal hair is one thing, but many contemporary wigmakers tend to be uneasy about using synthetic hair in their wigs. Most believe that, for the most realistic look, a wig must be made of healthy human hair. Although great progress has been made in engineering fibers, we are not yet able to replicate the properties of natural hair. For example, even in the best of synthetic wigs, the natural sheen is missing because of the absent cuticle. Synthetic fibers also melt at temperatures that natural hair can withstand, so wig handlers must use hair blowers with caution. And because they are made from plastics, synthetic hairs are also liable to be dissolved by the organic solvents used to remove adhesives, such as those holding a mustache or beard hairpiece in place.

Still, there are some advantages to synthetic hair. Synthetic fibers are clean, easily accessible in virtually any quantity, shape, thickness, or color, and relatively cheap. Because they are water-repellent, they are not affected by changes in humidity like natural hair. They're also particularly advantageous in situations when a wig can look like a wig and does not have to faithfully mirror nature. The wigmaker's creative skills are unlimited when he works with synthetic hair: The hairpiece may be of any color, thickness, length, kink, or curl—from a purple starburst, to a white curled, pile-upon-pile hair mountain, to a full, long tress discreetly covering a naked woman as she rides her horse through town.

There are some new synthetic fibers being developed for wig use, as I learned during a recent visit to the laboratories of Aderans Ltd, a billion-dollar Tokyo-based company that makes and sells wigs serving about 40 percent of the Japanese wig market.[4] There, engineers are currently developing more realistic synthetic fibers. One new fiber is actually a fiber within a fiber; the internal layering imparts to it greater tensile strength. Another fiber has a roughened surface that acts like a cuticle, in that *reflected* light gives a more natural luster. Still another fiber is able to take up water, giving it some of the curling properties of natural hair. Such engineering advances suggest that synthetic fibers will increasingly become part of the future cosmetic wig.

Whether the choice is for natural or synthetic material, once the hair fibers are selected, it's time to assemble the wig. The process begins on the wig block, which can be either a wooden or plastic model of a head. This, of course, is most often a generalization of an average head, though some specialty shops do make plastic molds that are exact replicas of their customers' heads. The block is covered with clear plastic wrap, upon which are lines giving the latitude and longitude of the head. The dimensions of the block establish the size and thus the fitting of the wig. If the wig is too loose, it will slip; if it is too tight, it will be intolerable to wear for a length of time.

The head block is covered with a wig net (also called the wig base or foundation), to which the wig hair will be tied. The net is composed of fine threads meant to simulate hair shafts. In portions of the wig where hair density would be low, such as the edge of the wig, the net threads are nearly invisible, made of either very fine silk, transparent synthetic fiber, or hair itself; in other areas, where hair growth would be denser, the net consists of thicker, stronger threads that can support more hair fibers. The net's threads form diamondlike arrays into which hair fibers are tied, one by one. One wig requires from thirty to forty thousand individual hairs, and, depending on the method used, a skilled wigmaker can assemble one wig within two weeks.

There are two ways of binding hairs onto the foundation. In the first way, individual hairs are tied directly onto the threads of the net using a knotting needle and either single or double knots. The way that individual hairs are tied into the net has a major impact on how the individual hairs fall—to the right, left, front, back—so the direction must be changed depending on the location on the head. The second way of binding hairs is by using wefts, or tracks. A weft looks something like a clothesline crammed with hairs hanging out to dry. The weft is convenient because it can be rapidly and inexpensively mass-produced in a factory; the wigmaker then sews into and covers the foundation with multiple wefts. Wefts work well in regions where hair density is high and the ribbed pattern of the weft will not be seen, such as on the top and back of the scalp; however, wefts do not work well in areas of thin hair or wig edges. The secret to weaving a good wig is to capture the subtle variations in the lay and character of normal hair, including hair partings, swirls, and cowlicks, without showing the stitches. One particular challenge is to make the wig margins look like a normal hairline composed of thin, singly placed, lightly pigmented hairs growing in low density. One trick is to place bangs or long hair strands over the sides and nape in order to mask the sharp, weft-produced border. The other dead giveaway of a wig is hair shaft uniformity, since any normal scalp has hair fibers varying in texture and color. To replicate the diversity of natural hair, the maker must incorporate hairs of different shades to mimic lighter-pigmented hairs on the crown, where sun would produce natural highlights, or even gray hairs at the temples.

Once the wig is fully knotted, a beautician will take over and coif the wig by cutting, curling, and dyeing it. Any ordinary beautician or barber will not do; it must be someone familiar with how wigs are made, because even a simple mistake, like combing the wig too deeply, could rip the foundation net and ruin the wig for good. The same care must be taken in maintenance; heavily used wigs must be washed, reset and, often, repaired on a defined schedule. In the theater world, the Actor's Equity union stipulates that a wig must be cleaned after every fourteen performances. Well-constructed and well-cared-for wigs may last for years, but, like all works of art, they need regular and tender care.

Upon hearing the word "wig," most people think of a covering for the head, but in fact hairpieces are not limited to the scalp. For example, in addition to designing head wigs for theatrical productions, Mawbey and his team are responsible for the facial hairpieces actors need: eyebrows, eyelashes, mustaches, goatees, sideburns, and full beards. Whether human, animal, or synthetic, the hair used for these constructs is coarser, shorter, and more curled than head hair. The wigmaker has to be aware that facial hair may differ in texture and color from the hair on the scalp; beard hair, for example, may be blonder, redder, or grayer.[5] Eyelashes are created with a weft made of short, heavily pigmented, slightly curled fibers, which is applied to the edge of the eyelid. Body hair—be it on arms, legs, or chest—can be embellished by means of hairnets with interwoven short, curled hairs. Even pubic hair can be created. The pubic wig, termed a merkin, dates back to medieval times, when prostitutes would shave their pubic hair in order to avoid lice, but then needed a cover for the marks of venereal diseases that would be visible on their bare skin. Today, actors quite frequently use them in film and onstage in order to avoid "indecent" genital exposure.

No matter where they appear on the body, wigs certainly aren't cheap. The price includes the cost of design, of hair or fiber, and of the long and tedious labor to knot it. Price can range widely—from $50 to $5,000 per wig. Further, many wig users must have at least several pieces on hand, which can be interchanged during time of cleaning and repair. Disposable wigs can somewhat reduce maintenance cost, but they're not as durable as more permanent wigs, and the user is committed to buying between four and twelve disposable units per year. And it all adds up. The size of the industry is difficult to value, since wigmaking is a fragmented process and there are many participants—hair merchants, wholesalers, fiber manufacturers, wig designers, wig-knotters, and wig beauticians. But workers in the field estimate that the total world market approaches $5 billion.[6]

Anyone who has watched an actor transform into a character onstage, or seen a loved one with hair loss beam with renewed confidence when wearing a wig, knows that wigs are magical. The simple act of donning one has the power to change a person. The people who design and make wigs are exceptional; like Mawbey, they are not only keen observers of nature but they are also insightful artists. But can hair apart be art?

QUEEN VICTORIA'S MEMENTO

*In 2007, a lock of President Abraham Lincoln's
hair sold for $11,095.*

O n October 25, 2007, the Heritage Auction Gallery of Dallas sold a strand of black hair taken from the dead body of revolutionary leader Che Guevara. The lone bidder—Bill Butler, a book dealer—paid an eye-popping $119,500 for the relic. At the time, Butler said he wanted to add a piece of this great leader to his collection of 1960s memorabilia. Earlier in the year, the same auction house had sold a lock of President Abraham Lincoln's hair for $11,095 and one of Confederate General J. E. B. Stuart's hair for $44,812. Hair from famous people commands high prices.[1] But why?

For collectors, hair houses the spirit of the person who grew it. By possessing the hair, collectors feel as if they own a tangible piece of that person. There are many different cultures—past and present—that believe hair houses a person's life force. References to the spirits embedded in hair both attached to and separated from the body are found in myth and culture.[2] For example, in Greek mythology, Mnemosyne, mother of the nine muses, stores her remarkable memory in her very long hair. In the Bible, Samson stored his strength not in his muscles but in his hair—so when his two-timing lover cut his hair, he lost his remarkable might and didn't recover it until his hair regrew. In Japanese tradition, the sumo wrestler's force resides in his hair; cutting a sumo's long hair during the retirement ceremony signals the end of his fighting career. Many people have believed that the essence of a person is connected to hair, and it was a common thought that wounding hair—even if detached from the body—could cause bodily harm. By this way of thinking, West African Yoruba people protect their cut hairs lest the spirit embedded in them come under the influence of a malefactor who could exploit them. Folklore from more than a few cultures has stories of demonic sorcerers (or sorceresses) who apply love potions to captured hairs in order to facilitate an unwanted seduction. Hair has also been used in votive offerings, as when Japanese women sacrificed locks of hair to shrines for the safe return of their loved ones, or when modern Indian women donate their hair to temples in expiation for their sins.

People have long cherished hair as memory pieces or religious relics, but the fascination grew in popularity at the time of the English Civil War following the execution of King Charles I. Citizens who had supported the king wore strands of the dead

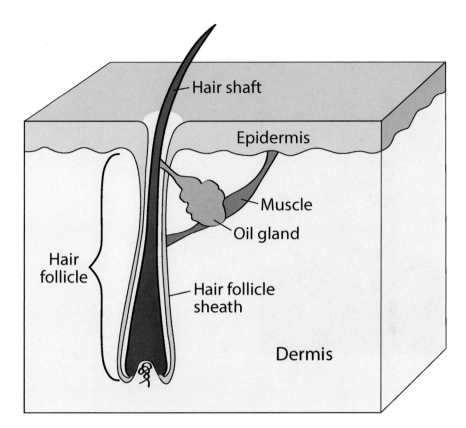

ABOVE: Line drawing of skin with central lying hair follicle. (*Art by Mark Saba, Yale University. Used with permission.*) LEFT: Control of cell growth in most biological systems occurs by means of an inhibitor neutralizing an inhibitor to the activator. Here is an analogy to help make the process clear: A UPS driver (the activator) wants to deliver a package. If a thug (an inhibitor) attacks him, he will not deliver the package, but if a police officer (the inhibitor neutralizing the inhibitor) restrains the thug, the UPS driver will proceed unimpeded. Similarly, multiple steps in cell growth regulation prevent growth where it is not needed (e.g. extra hair or, worse, cancer cells). (*Art by Mark Saba, Yale University. Used with permission.*)

LEFT: The newborn nimbus. Before the first hair shafts are heavy enough to fall, they stand straight up, a once-in-a-lifetime halo. (*Used with permission from by Greg Burnham.*) BELOW: The hair follicle growth cycle. As long as a person lives, her hair follicles cycle, forming hair shafts and then shedding them. (*Art by Mark Saba, Yale University. Used with permission.*)

Hair Follicle Growth Cycle
from Anagen to Anagen

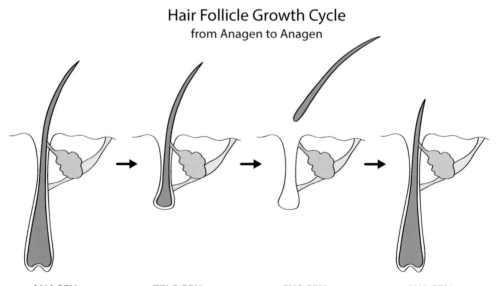

ANAGEN	**TELOGEN**	**EXOGEN**	**ANAGEN**
Growing hair follicle and shaft	Resting hair follicle and non-growing shaft	Shedding the shaft	Regrowing hair follicle and new shaft

RIGHT: Even the great Julius Caesar was concerned with his balding. Note that the sculptor faithfully portrayed the comb-over which historians described. (*Photograph by Musée Arles Antique. Distributed under a CC BY-SA 3.0 license.*) BELOW: Patterns of male pattern balding. Hamilton recognized that hair loss occurred in predictable arrangements. (*Reprinted with permission from J. B. Hamilton's "Patterned Loss of Hair in Man,"* The Annals of the New York Academy of Science, *53:712, 1951.* © *The New York Academy of Sciences.*)

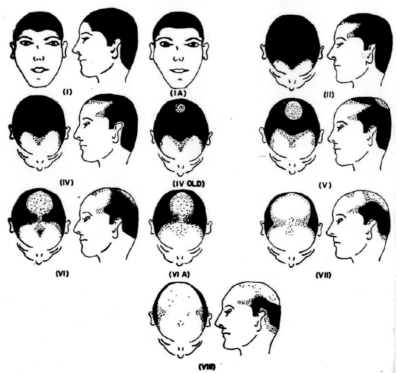

FIGURE 1. Sketches of the categories of scalp hairiness which were set up for classification and grading of the extent of common baldness. The categories or types of scalp are described in the text and illustrated in FIGURES 2 to 15 by photographs of subjects. In scalp Types I, II, and III, the loss of hair is insufficient to qualify as baldness. Types IV, V, VI, VII, and VIII represent a graded progression of common baldness. No sketch of Type III is included in FIGURE 1 because of the variety of conditions that constitute Type III.

ABOVE LEFT AND RIGHT: Hair defines the person. A silhouette of hair alone is enough to identify Margaret Thatcher and Ronald Reagan. (*Used with permission from Christina Christoforou's* Whose Hair, *Laurence King Publishing, 2011.*) BELOW LEFT AND RIGHT: Gibson Girl (right) and bobbed hair (left). (*Art by Charles Dana Gibson [right] and Mark Saba, Yale University [left]. Used with permission.*)

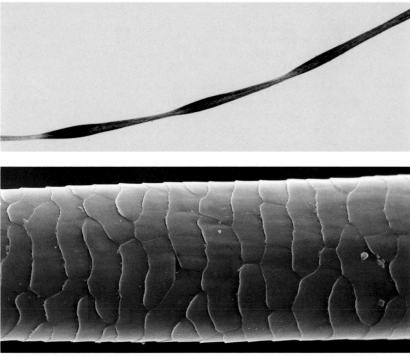

TOP: *Barbershop of 19th century America.* An African American-owned business in Alexandria, 1816–1877. As depicted in this sketch, the barbers were black and the customers white. (*Image by Eyre Crowe from "Illustrated London News," 38:207, March 9, 1861. Used with permission from Special Collections, University of Virginia Library, Charlottesville.*) CENTER: Monilethrix hair showing pearl necklace shape of the shaft as a result of an abnormal or absent hair shaft protein (keratin). (*Used with permission from Professor Antonella Tosti, University of Miami.*) BOTTOM: Mouse hair shaft with its shingle-like cuticle. The hair shaft tip is to the left in this picture. Because of the way cuticle cells cover the shaft, its surface is rougher when you rub it from top to bottom than from bottom to top. (*Used with permission from J. P. Sundberg, Jackson Laboratory, Maine.*)

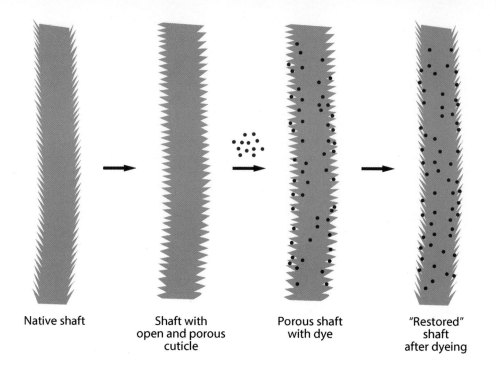

| Native shaft | Shaft with open and porous cuticle | Porous shaft with dye | "Restored" shaft after dyeing |

ABOVE: Steps in dyeing a hair shaft. To place dye into a hair shaft, the hair stylist opens the cuticle, makes the shaft permeable, adds dye, and finally restores the shaft and closes the cuticle. (*Art by Mark Saba, Yale University. Used with permission.*) BELOW: Wigmaker's tools: wig block plus a net and a ribbon of hairs called a weft. The wigmaker adds hair to the net either individually or as a weft, which may be factory-made. (*Art by Mark Saba, Yale University. Used with permission.*)

Wig Block
with wig net
(foundation)

Weft
(string with hair strands)

RIGHT: The Macaroni. These fops used the wig in extreme; notice where he placed his hat. (*Reprinted with permission from Hulton Archive, Getty Images.*) BELOW: *UN-1, United Nations—The Babel of the Millennium*, by Gu Wenda. The large sculpture pictured here comes from the artist's United Nation series. In this series, it is the artist's goal to collect hairs from peoples around the world and blend them into one work. Decorating the screen tower are pseudo Chinese, English, Hindi, and Arabic words sketched using donor hair. (*Used with permission from Gu Wenda.*)

TOP LEFT: Modifications of the beaver hat. The beaver pelt market was based on the demand for hats and the style ranged widely. (*Image from Horace T. Martin's* Castorologia, Or, The History and Traditions of the Canadian Beaver, *W. M. Drysdale & Co., 1892.*) TOP RIGHT: Scissors for sheep shearing (*Photo by Andreas Praefcke, public domain.*) BOTTOM RIGHT: Etching of wool merchant John Fortey, Northleach Church. Fortey's right foot rests on a sheep and his left on a sack of wool, acknowledging the source of his great wealth. (*Used with permission from Julia Owen and Simon Wills of Northleach Church, Cotswolds.*)

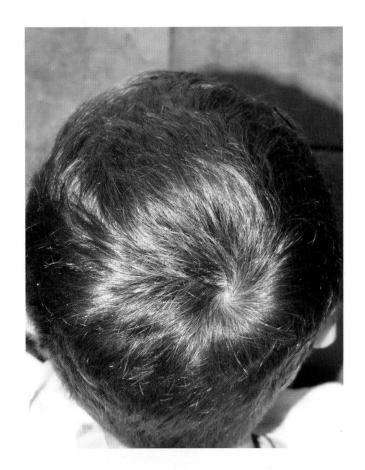

ABOVE: Scalp hair cowlick of left-handed ten-year-old boy. Notice that the hairs lie predominantly in a counterclockwise position. (*Used with permission from K. Svoboda.*) BELOW: *Birth of Venus*, Sandro Botticelli, 1485. Iconic female beauty: copious scalp hair but nothing on the body. (*Used with permission from Uffizi Gallery, Florence.*)

ABOVE: Dreadlocks. Forming locks depends on the felting properties of human hair and its shaft cuticle. (*Used with permission from Professor Andrew Alexis, MD, MPH, Department of Dermatology, Mount Sinai St. Luke's Hospital.*) BOTTOM LEFT: *Woman Combing Her Hair*, ca. 1888–1890, by Edgar Degas. Even the apparently benign process of hair combing can damage the cuticle and hair shaft. (*Used with permission from the Metropolitan Museum of Art, New York.*) BOTTOM RIGHT: An Eighteenth Century Barbershop. *The Barber*, by Marcellus Laroon the Younger, 1679 – 1772. (*Courtesy of the Yale Center for British Art.*)

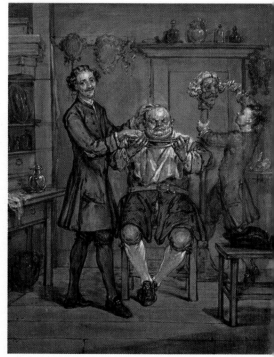

Mourning jewelry, also called *memento mori*. All components of this sculpture are made of hair, including the willow branches and mausoleum. (*From the collection of Leila Cohoon; photograph by Adam Green. Used with permission.*)

ABOVE: Family wreath hair sculpture. Each family member contributed his or her hair to the artist, who placed them in the shape of a wreath. (*From the collection of Leila Cohoon; photograph by Adam Green. Used with permission.*) BELOW LEFT AND RIGHT: *Cornrow Chair*, 2011 and *Black Hair Flag*, 2010. The ironic use of African American hair in symbols of the Confederate South underscores the integral and inextricable role of black slaves in that society. (*By artist Sonya Clark. From the collection of the Virginia Museum of Fine Arts. Photograph by Taylor Dabney. Used with permission.*)

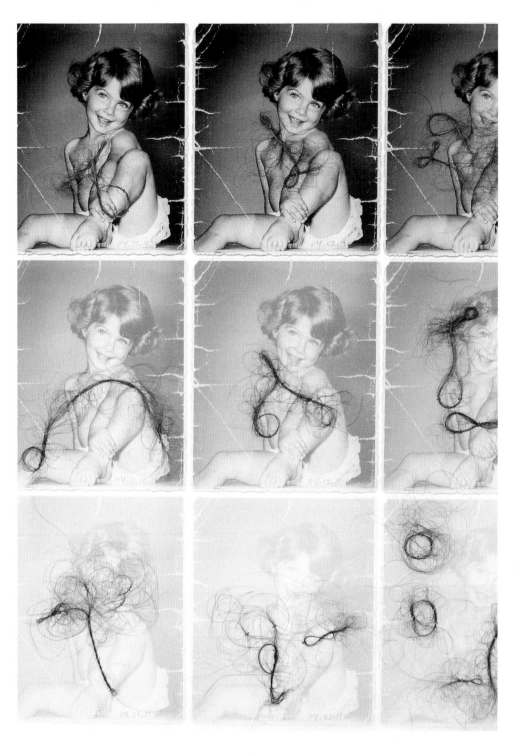

A Question of Beauty No. 2: April 2011. The permanence of hair as youth and life fades harkens back to the enduring value of hair in mourning jewelry. (*Used with permission from artist Babs Reingold.*)

LEFT: *Untitled 1990* by Tom Friedman depicts a sculpture bar of white soap with inlaid spirals of the artist's pubic hair. (*Used with permission from artist Luhring Augustine and Stephen Friedman Gallery, London.*)

CENTER: Beaver pelt consists of small, fine fibers making up the underfur (lower portion of photo) and long, straight, coarse fibers making up the overfur (upper portion of photo). (*Author's collection; Beaver pelt provided by Alan Herscovici, Fur Council of Canada.*)

LEFT: Hudson Bay blanket. Pictured is one of the several blankets the Hudson Bay Company used to barter with the Indian fur traders. (*Author's collection.*)

ABOVE: *Carding*, by Maria Wilk, 1883. The carder combed wool by transferring it from one card to the other until the bundle of wool transferred consisted of parallel fibers. (*http://www.fromsheeptoshawl. com/wp-content/uploads/2012/06/Maria-Wilk- Girl-Carding-Wool.jpg*) LEFT: Fuller's Teasel. The dried fruit of the teasel plant was used to comb wool well before the ancient Greek-Roman times. (*Photograph by Didier Descouens. Distributed under a CC BY-SA 4.0 license.*)

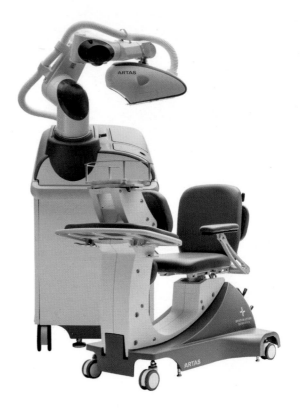

TOP LEFT: *The Spinner*, a painting by William-Adolphe Bouguereau from 1873, shows a girl with a wool-filled distaff in her left arm and a wool thread and spindle in her right hand. She pulls strands of wool from the distaff, twists them slightly, and attaches the strand to the spinning spindle. (*http://www.wikiart.org/en/william-adolphe-bouguereau/the-spinner-1873*) TOP RIGHT: *Bear with Me*. This miniature painting (see penny in the upper left for scale) illustrates how a gifted artist using fine hair brushes can reproduce hair itself. (*Used with permission from artist Linda Rossin.*) BOTTOM RIGHT: Hair transplant robot. The robot identifies hair follicles, removes them, and then makes incision sites on the scalp for implantation. (*ARTAS® System. Used with permission from Restoration Robotics, Inc.*)

regent's hair in their jewelry as a token of mourning as well as a declaration of political affiliation. Soon, the custom spread beyond the monarchy to people making a similar kind of mourning jewelry for their own loved ones. These so-called *memento mori* pieces (Latin for "remember you must die") typically consisted of a gold locket suspended on a black velvet band. The face of the locket contained a tress of hair from a loved one in a design representing some symbol of death, such as a small coffin, skeleton, hourglass, or gravedigger's shovel. Inscribed in the locket center was the deceased's name. One of the most famous celebrants of the *memento mori* tradition was England's Queen Victoria. Not only did she enjoy a long rule during the grandest time of the British Empire but she also had an unusual marriage, as royal marriages go. Her consort was Albert of Saxe-Coburg and Gotha, a well-educated, innovative, and progressive scholar who was also her indispensable adviser. When he died in 1861, Victoria fell into a long and deep period of mourning. Although she never fully overcame the loss, she found some consolation in keeping Albert's hair close to herself in lockets, pendants, and rings.

Perhaps inspired by Victoria, 18th-century American women treasured the spiritual properties of hair. To them, clipped hair was used to convey messages of friendship, love, mourning, and family bonds. They kept hair of loved ones close to their everyday life by means of the jewelry they wore, on framed works hanging from their walls, and in albums on their desks and shelves. Martha Washington, an avid devotee of hair jewelry, took hair from state visitors and fashioned them into lockets or frames.[3] Abigail Adams, wife of the second U.S. president, John Adams, had a brooch and stick pin containing hairs from herself, her husband, and her son, John Quincy Adams, the sixth U.S. president. Victorian poet Robert Browning wore a gold ring containing his and his wife's entwined hair. On the band was the inscription "Ba" and the engraving "God Bless You, June 29, 1861," the day his wife, Elizabeth Barrett Browning, died.[4]

But hair locks have long signified more than just friendship, family bonds, or mourning. An exchange of hair has been meaningful in romantic relationships—though in many different ways. In some cases, when a shy young man asked a woman for a hair lock, he was actually initiating a marriage proposal. However, it is also true that some lotharios—with very little intent on marriage—kept tresses to record conquests. Additionally, women have used hair as a seduction tool. In fact, Lady Caroline Lamb flaunted her on-again-off-again affair with Lord Byron by sending him a tress of her pubic hair in a gold locket bearing a miniature portrait of Byron.[5] There is no record of what he did with it; we do know, however, that he stopped seeing Caroline shortly thereafter.

As long as a relationship thrived, a person proudly wore his lover's hair, but once passions cooled, the hair-gift took on a different aspect. Consider "The Funeral," written in 1633 by British poet John Donne. In the poem, the rejected lover requests that "WHOEVER comes to shroud me, do not harm,/ Nor question much, That subtle wreath of hair, which crowns my arm." The hair encircling his arm comes from a lady who now refuses him. The poem is not explicit about why the lover bestowed hair on the narrator in the first place, but we can assume there had been serious lovemaking (or at least intentions thereof) in the past. In the last line, he scornfully adds, "That since you would have none of me, I bury some of you." To this rejected lover, hair is more than symbolic of his love; it's a real part of her and, in the end, he has his vengeance.

To create these hair mementos, people most often simply collected a lock of hair (either from themselves or from a deceased or living person with whom they had a deep personal attachment), cleaned it in boiling water, dried it, and then shaped it or tied it in artistic arrangements. In some cases, the hair was pulverized, mixed with a glue, and used as a form of paint to fashion the ornament. People also placed hair in letters and albums using creative and intricate designs with adjacent expressions of love in the form of poems, essays, or drawings.

Although hair art started as an inexpensive gesture that all might enjoy, it ultimately became the purview of mostly middle-class women who had the luxury of time to develop both the craft and the close friends with whom they shared it. By the mid-19th century, the demand for hair art grew to such an extent that many women sought the help of professional artists to do the work. With the introduction of professionals, the art became more widely available and the messages became less personal and more commercial. It did not, however, become cheaper. For those who bought it, professionally made hair jewelry was expensive. An 1855 issue of *Godey's Magazine and Lady's Book* advertised mourning necklaces ranging in cost from four to seven dollars each at a time when the average wealth per capita in the United States was a little over $300.[6] By the late 19th century, the ardor for hair jewelry faded, in part because women had new opportunities outside the home as well as another vehicle for recording one's physical self: photography. By the start of the 20th century, interest in *memento mori* pieces had stopped almost entirely, viewed as morbid, sentimental, and just plain old-fashioned.

The largest known hair collection from this era is located in Independence, Missouri, quartered in a simple, one-storied, tan brick building along a main highway. Leila's Hair Museum consists of three large rooms, each with framed artworks covering the walls and glass-sided exhibit chests filling the floors. The founder,

Leila Cohoon, is a former hair stylist and salon owner who started collecting hair art more than sixty years ago when, on her way shoe shopping, she passed an antique store displaying a framed hair sculpture. Her shoe money—$135—went to buy the sculpture instead. Cohoon continues to build her collection by acquiring hair art from wherever she can find it: antique sales, auctions, garage sales, and by word of mouth.[7]

The Cohoon collection contains hair sculptures and multiple different forms of jewelry in which hair is incorporated into watch fobs, earrings, lockets, pendants, rings, brooches, and pins. The largest pieces are framed "wreath" sculptures. Very typical of this presentation is Cohoon's first piece: a wall hanging, five inches by five inches with gold frame, in which a dirty-blond hair tress sits in the center shaped as a horseshoe made of overlapping leaflike hair clusters. The back of the piece is signed from "Mamma and Papa." These "wreath" sculptures were quite popular. Typically each family member donated one leaf made of his or her hair and then the artist wrote the name of the person and relationship adjacent to the leaf as a kind of family tree. After all family members had contributed, the artist closed the circle to complete the wreath.

In recent years, a new generation of sculptors has taken up hair as a medium for their artistic expression far beyond the constructs of *memento mori* jewelry. While most people are accustomed to seeing animal hair as a neutral medium in a piece of art, the use of actual human hair becomes an integral part of the artistic meaning. Unlike paper, wood, paint, clay, stone, bronze, metals, and plastics, human hair comes from a living, thinking, laughing, crying human body, and so its use as a material raises the immediate question: Who gave the hair and why? Hair artist Cassandra Holden[8] asserts that "people are often uncomfortable seeing hair that is unattached to a human body because of its intense personal nature."

There are many different applications for hair in art.[9] One of the most basic uses is demonstrated by artist Althea Murphy-Price, who sculpts free hair into shapes. Terry Boddie takes the message-sending properties of hair quite literally by creating words with letters made of hair. In her work "A Question of Beauty," Babs Reingold juxtaposes the fading photograph of a child with an unchanging golden lock of hair from that child, contrasting the impermanence of life with the permanence of hair. In "Untitled 1990," Tom Friedman displayed his pubic hairs embedded in a plain white bar of soap. In another piece, artist Sanya Clark incorporated African hair into the fabric of a Confederate flag and house chair, underscoring the structural presence of African people in the society of that time.

These are just a few of the vast number of artworks that use human hair as a medium. In exploiting an intensely personal item—perhaps one of the most intimate pieces of the body—these artists make weighty statements with overarching philosophic, social, political, and moral meanings. These and the *memento mori* pieces show that hair off the body can send just as powerful a message as hair on the body.

All the stakeholders of the story up to now have been concerned with the nature of hair and the signals it sends. The next group of people is interested in how hair can serve human needs. We start with some of the bravest and most daring of this group: the fur trappers, traders, and explorers who sought beaver for an insatiable European market.

PART THREE

~

IN HUMAN SERVICE

CHAPTER 11

QUEST FOR BEAVER MAPS A CONTINENT

—

*Because of the cyclic nature of hair growth, there is only
one time of the year when fur can be harvested.*

J ust as important to the story of hair as the stuff on our heads
and bodies is the animal hair we have used to cover ourselves.
Humans needed some sort of body cover when they migrated
out of Africa approximately one hundred thousand years ago[1] into
climates requiring protection from wind and cold. Initially, the
most accessible cover consisted of the skins left over from food kill,

and so the coats of humans' prey became their own. Any animal skin would do, but the climate and the most accessible mammals within the hunting range dictated the choice. Humans adopted the skins pretty much as they found them: After removing the adherent tissues, they dried the skins, softened them, and, straightaway, wore them.

Early humans collected skins from the animals they hunted, but the job got a lot easier about nine thousand years ago when humans learned to herd. This landmark event reduced, and in some regions obviated, the need to hunt for food and skins. Husbanded animals provided the pelt (defined as skin plus fur): leather from cows and pigs and furred skin from sheep and goats. Unfortunately, the most highly prized and richly furred animals were not easily domesticated; these animals lived in a cold, harsh, northern habitat where survival in the winter depended on an efficient surface cover.

Throughout the Classical period and thereafter, people from the thriving Greek, Roman, and Arabic societies of the Mediterranean basin demanded wild animal furs of all sorts, and natives living in the cold forests of northern Europe, Scandinavia, and Russia supplied them. By the mid-8th century—even before the dawn of Viking invasions—the Swedes operated settlements along the eastern Baltic Sea coast where they met and traded with Western Europeans and Arabic merchants, who traveled northward along the Volga and Don Rivers. The Arabs sought slaves and fur and the Vikings in turn wanted high-quality Arabian silver and silver coins. This trade (when the Scandinavians did trade and not plunder) in part motivated the Swedish Vikings to push farther east and south, to pass through the gates of Constantinople, and to tap directly into its market. These Rus Vikings assimilated easily, leaving behind a historical imprint with the fusion of two great cultures and the genetic blue-eyed heritage of generations to come.

In the later Middle Ages, the Crusaders returned home from their lofty campaigns to the Holy Land with impressions of a new life enjoyed by the stylish inhabitants of Islam; their image included decorative furs. The major fur suppliers to this new western market continued to be the hunters and trappers from Scandinavia, eastern Germany, Russia, and Siberia. Transporting furs (which included sable, ermine, fox, marten, otter, and squirrel) to the medieval market towns was no easy chore, not only because of perilous shipping routes and poor roads, but also because of highway bandits. To develop this trade, a secure distribution system was critical. One agency that championed links between the markets of the West and the suppliers of northeastern Europe was the Order of the Teutonic Knights of St. Mary's Hospital in Jerusalem.

The Teutonic Knights, a military organization associated with the Roman Catholic Church, was founded primarily to protect and aid Christians on their pilgrimage to the Holy Land. Embracing the religious fervor of that era, the knights also took it upon themselves to Christianize the peoples of Eastern Europe by using what they knew best: military tactics. During their heyday between the 12th and 15th centuries, the Teutonic Knights accrued great wealth in part by buying furs from the east, transporting them along a chain of fur-trading forts extending from the Volga River north to the Baltic Sea, and then selling them to western markets in Europe and England.

Fur trade was important to the English economy from its earliest times, and in support of the commerce, King Edward II established a guild in London in 1327 named "Worshipful Company of Skinners." Since the royal policy encouraged English merchants to seek the best price, in 1408, Henry IV empowered a company of English merchants to bargain with the various importing groups, presumably including the Teutonic Knights. One century later, though, the king thought he could do even better: Henry VIII instructed his fur merchants to circumvent the large traders and negotiate directly with the Russian tsar, Ivan IV, for English fur imports.

The furs that European and Arab traders cherished were, in general, not meant for practical or casual purposes; they were meant to wear and strut. Because furs were used to distinguish the strata of society, the ruling classes enacted sumptuary laws limiting fur access and use. King Edward III enforced laws defining who could wear which fur: one specific fur for kings, another for nobles, yet another for the high clergy, and so on. In many countries, the use of sable was limited to the position of king, for example. Even as late as the 16th century, German states enforced sumptuary laws stating that the noble furs—marten and ermine—were not to be worn by merchants despite their growing wealth and influence. And while the middle classes could wear lamb, fox, weasel, and other cheap pelts, common citizens could not wear any fur at all.

Though exotic furs of all sorts were favored to decorate the robes of royalty, nobility, clergy, and rich merchants, the fur of greatest demand in 16th-century European society was beaver. For generations, Europeans had prized the beaver for its thick fur coat of short, very fine hair fibers. Most of the demand for beaver fur stemmed from a hat. In the 16th century, a proper beaver hat was *de rigueur* for both established and aspiring gentlemen. Such hats were the symbols of status and wealth, worn outdoors, indoors, at church, and at the dinner table. The hats came in many different styles—broad or narrow, rimmed or straight, high or flat, bejeweled or plain—and they were all relatively expensive. Samuel Pepys, the famed 17th-century London diarist and spendthrift, groused that he had to put out 1 percent of his yearly salary for his "bever."[2]

In fact, these beaver hats were so valuable they were often left as a bequest in wills.

These hats were expensive because they took a great deal of work. One production step involved the cuticle; because beaver hair cuticle is not prominent, hatters found they had to open the cuticle in order to achieve optimal felting. One such treatment, carrotting (named for the color it imparted to the fur tips), required the application of mercury salts to the hairs. While the mercury salts effectively flared the cuticle cells and facilitated the felting process, the fumes generated were highly toxic to the workers. The exposed hatter often developed symptoms of severe mercury neurotoxicity, including a lurching gait, difficulty speaking, distorted vision, and confusion. (This toxicity was so common to the trade that the phrase "mad as a hatter" arose, a condition not as jolly as the tea party in Lewis Carroll's *Alice's Adventures in Wonderland* would suggest.) After carrotting, the fibers were shaved or plucked from the skin, felted, molded into a hat shape, and then re-felted. Finally, the hat was soaked in a stiffening solution containing vinegar, chestnut leaves, and glue. Most hats were dyed black and, in some cases, they were waterproofed with resin, beeswax, or suet. In the end, after stiffening, the hats were very hard: It was said that they were so stiff they could support a two-hundred-pound man. They were also extremely long-lasting and virtually everyone who was anyone wanted one.

Unfortunately, while demand for beaver fur was growing, its supply was fading. Centuries of intense hunting and habitat destruction had exhausted furred animal populations in Northern European forests. By the early 17th century, the beaver population was essentially extinct in Western Europe and severely depleted in the Scandinavian-Baltic-Russian streams and forests. But there were rumors of a fresh supply in the forests of the New World, and so they set sail to find it.

The American beaver trade began on the North American shore. Off the coast of the continent between Cape Cod and Nova Scotia is the Georges Bank, a large submarine ridge that, because of tidal mixing, is one of the most biologically productive waters in the world. These nutrient-rich waters supported the growth of huge schools of feed fish such as herring, haddock, and cod, and the fish attracted European fishermen. In order to preserve their catch, on every trip fishermen spent weeks to months air-drying and/or salting fish on shore. Occasionally, they were met by fur-clad people willing to trade the pelts they were wearing for Western decorative trinkets, metal items, or cloth. At first this trade was merely an extra dividend for the fishermen who braved the long voyage, but, with time, they realized the value this exchange engendered; what had started as a casual barter became a business of its own, much more lucrative than the hook and net. Stories filtered back to Europe about a land rich with fur; rumors claimed more than 50 million beaver and other fur-bearing animals lived in the forests of North America between the Atlantic and Pacific oceans, from the Arctic tundra to the Gulf of California.[3] The fur was there for the taking. Thus was launched the two-hundred-year "Gold Rush" of that era.

Dutch, Swedish, English, and, to a lesser extent, Spanish settlers participated in and benefited from this highly profitable trade, but Canadian-French traders were both the earliest and the most successful. Native Americans traded with the Europeans as well as with one another. Because of territorial and cultural barriers, negotiations between the two sides of this market were challenging, and rivalries within each side flared frequently. Due to the many different parties and interests, the complete story of the fur trade in North America is complex, filled with conflicts and clashes, the formation and break-up of confederations, the boom and bust of markets and the building and destruction of settlements and societies.

The original trade consisted of an irregular exchange of materials between two groups of merchants: the Native Americans, who caught and brought furs, and the Europeans, who manufactured and brought trade items. With time, the rendezvous became defined and anticipated. The first documented port of exchange was at Tadoussac on the northern coast of the St. Lawrence River, followed by upstream trading forts at Quebec, Trois Rivières, and Montreal. Although archeological evidence of the first trades is scant and uncertain, a few European-made decorative items found in the soil of these areas suggest that material exchanges were ongoing in the late 1500s.[4] New World furs traveled from hand to hand eastward, and European trade items traveled from business to business westward. Both groups of traders were dependent on a complex concatenation of middlemen from shore to deep continent and back. The Huron, Iroquois, Susquehanna, Powhatan, and Cherokee were the great middlemen in the early Eastern fur trade, trapping, buying, and looting beaver from the interior and carrying it to others on its way to the East Coast ports.

Communication and bartering among Native Americans appear to have been in force well before the arrival of the Europeans, so news regarding rewards from the earliest trades spread rapidly from tribal unit to tribal unit across North America.[5] Samuel Champlain, the 17th-century French explorer and founder of Quebec City, noted that an intracontinental fur commerce was already quite active on his arrival in 1603. The same observation was made by Europeans who traveled farther west to the shores of James Bay (a finger of Hudson Bay) in 1611.

The Native American hunter knew the beaver's habits well, including the fact that castoreum, a perianal gland secretion from the beaver, was very attractive to others of its species and could be used as a universal bait. To catch a beaver, the hunter would coat a twig with castoreum and then wait for his prey to arrive. Native Americans had historically clubbed or lanced the beaver, but they soon began to use the European-brought metal traps, which were placed near the entrance of the beaver's lodge. When a beaver stepped onto the device, the trap's jaws clamped onto its leg. The startled beaver's first response was to dive into deep water, but as it jumped, it pulled the weighted trap along. The hunter would then collect the drowned animal the next morning.

In the early trade, the beaver was skinned at the site of trapping. The carcass was placed on its back, hands and feet were removed, a cut was made along the belly from chin to tail, and the pelt was peeled off as if removing a coat. The trapper brought the pelt back to his settlement where it was processed further by the women of his community. They removed the flesh and fat by scraping the pelt with a flat stone, sharpened bone, or shell, taking great care to make sure they preserved the hair roots. The cleaned pelts were then stretched on U-shaped tree branches and air-dried for several weeks. After that, the stiff pelt was softened by applying a concoction of alkaline ash, animal fat, and brain extracts and then by massaging and beating it. The last step was to remove the overhairs, which are long, coarse hairs extending beyond the short, fine hairs of the deep fur. Most often, the overhairs were plucked out by hand, though they could also be removed by wearing the pelt inside out. Traders referred to these worn skins as "made beaver" because the fur was ready for immediate use. The treated pelts were then packed into canoes and taken to the next broker in the series of brokers traveling east until meeting the ultimate European trader and his ocean-faring vessels.

Traditionally, Native Americans took only what they could use for food and clothing. Later, they disregarded their traditions and better judgment for the European enticements, taking as many animals as they thought they could trade. To increase their yield, trappers would sometimes dismantle a whole lodge and then kill the exposed beaver family, regardless of age or sex, with club, lance, or gun. By the 1840s, the beaver population in North American forests dropped, as had happened in European forests three hundred years earlier, and the beaver fur trade collapsed.

Until that point, the hunt for beaver crept progressively and inexorably westward, driven by the promise of better furs from animals living in the colder western and more northern climes, but also by the depletion of the eastern stock. By means of this drive for fur—back and forth from the source to the market, from the market and trade items to the fur source—the fur traders, following in the footsteps of the Native Americans, mapped the continent for the European settlement that was to come. One cannot over-state the importance of the beaver in catalyzing the first map of North America; a beaver image on the Canadian five-cent coin commemorates its significance.

The growing market for products in the New World galvanized and expanded multiple European industries. On the one hand, processing beaver pelts required multiple industries going from pelt to hat: from transporting bundles of pelt along the St. Lawrence River to European cities and factories, to processing the fur, and finally to distributing the finished product to the market. On the other hand, items used to trade for fur had to be manufactured: These included metal tools, guns, ammunition, pots, and utensils, as well as rum, glass trinkets, and woven goods such as blankets. Both sides of the trade also impacted the banking industry as set-tlers, trappers, and traders needed capital to get started. In so many ways, the fur trade was as much an economic stimulus in Europe as it was in North America.

Today, the people using fur and the workers supplying it are not without their critics, of course. Since the late 1960s, there has been a growing opposition to the use of fur in general but also to fur hunting and fur farming specifically. There are two camps in this regard. One group maintains that any use of animal skin is unethical. Countries such as Austria and Switzerland, in fact, have passed laws prohibiting animal fur farms altogether. The second group accepts the use of animal products for human use but asserts that a higher standard of animal care must be practiced. The fur industry has generated guidelines such as "Best Management Practices" aimed to improve animal handling on farms and to assure humane treatment of animals captured in the wild. Groups sympathetic to the pelt industry have argued that hunting animals in the wild is a "green" method for controlling animal populations in a shrinking habitat.[6]

Yet fur is still in demand. Today, 85 percent of the world's fur production is derived from farm-raised animals, and most of that comes from Europe. More than three hundred mink farms exist in the United States and they produce about three million pelts annually. Global sales for furs totaled $40 billion in 2012–2013, with particularly large and expanding markets in China and Russia.[7] Industrialists credit the expanding markets to more accessible pricing and to a greater acceptance of furs in a variety of social situations; people wear furs today not only at formal dress affairs, such as cotillion balls, but also at more casual occasions such as spectator sporting events.

Early in history, humans recognized they could enjoy the benefits of fur without sacrificing the animal. The next hair workers are the craftspeople who have converted shaved hair into cloth: the wool workers.

12

WOOL BANKROLLS AN EMPIRE

—

Wool made the fortunes of many who handled it, including Cosimo de' Medici, the famous Renaissance banker, and Christopher Columbus.

P erhaps the most famous weaver of wool was Penelope, queen of Ithaca. As Homer's epic poem *The Odyssey* opens, Penelope is weeping over the absence of her husband, Odysseus, the storied warrior and king who left her twenty years earlier to join the Greek states in their campaign against Troy. Although she heard he had survived the war and started homeward, she knew nothing more. Was he returning? Imprisoned? Dead? The uncertainty of

Odysseus's fate presented an irreconcilable dilemma to Penelope. In the society of her day, as long as a woman's husband lived, she had the obligation to preserve his home; on the other hand, if her husband was dead, she was equally obliged to remarry. What should she do? Penelope conceded that as soon as she finished weaving a shroud for Odysseus's aged father, Laertes, she would choose a husband from among her multiple suitors. So, from sunrise to sundown, she wove cloth, and then every night, she furtively unraveled it. After three years, when the suitors finally discovered her ruse, they were furious and swore to murder Telemachus, Penelope's son and Odysseus's heir. As the story ends, Odysseus returns home and defeats the seditious suitors to reclaim his kingdom and reunite his family at last.

When faced with crushing social pressure, Penelope took refuge in the work she had known all her life: the spinning and weaving of wool. This is hardly surprising, since wool was women's work, and its product—cloth—was critical to the household. Wool work filled the free hours of every Greek woman—commoner or queen—and Homer writes of women who spun fleece every day from before sunrise until well after dusk. And so it's no surprise that Penelope turned to this familiar activity in her time of need.

The story of wool encompasses nothing less than the history of civilization. Up until about three hundred years ago, few children grew up without some knowledge of spinning yarn, warping a loom, or passing a shuttle through a shed. The ways of wool were embedded in nearly every aspect of human existence back then, and our language bears witness to that exposure. Consider how many wool-based metaphors we use, most likely without any thought of their origins, among them "fabric of life," "unraveling a mystery," "on tenterhooks," "homespun ideas," "my spinster aunt," "heirloom," "to spin a yarn," "weavers of long tales," "thread of an argument," and "space shuttle." But as wool has been important to many cultures over many times, the subject is so huge that no single chapter—let alone a single book—could render a balanced description of its rich history. But one important aspect of that larger story can be seen by examining the wool trade in medieval England.

During the Middle Ages, wool became the foundation and driver of the social, political, economic, and industrial development of the British Empire. The earliest British inhabitants herded sheep and processed wool; in fact, when the Romans invaded England in 43 C.E., they already found wool-working to be an important feature of that society. Not only were sheep grazing throughout the land, but Englishmen were spinning high-quality wool and weaving cloth that was "so fine it was comparable with a spider's web."[1]

During the 12th century, cloth-making was a cottage industry. The simplest system of wool production occurred on a homestead where the family cultivated and manufactured all its material needs: grain for food, wood or peat for heat, and wool for cloth. If the farmer generated more wool than he needed, he would trade or sell it to his neighbors in exchange for other materials. As demand increased and the farmer became more skilled in cloth-making, he progressively reduced his time tending crops and spent more time working with wool.

Later, these specialized tradesmen formed guilds, which possessed king-granted-authority to define, protect, and regulate the wool market. In London, the first weaver's guild formed in 1130. The guild worker owned both the raw materials (wool) and the instruments of production (weaving looms). As time went by and cloth manufacturing became more efficient, the cottager-weaver began using outside agents or merchants to supply wool. The farmer transferred the uncertainties of wool production to someone else. In this domestic system, the tradesman worked at home using his own tools but with raw materials supplied by another investor. In the course of the Middle Ages, all three forms of production were active: cottage, guild, and domestic. (The factory system developed later than our story, ushering in the Industrial Revolution of the 18th century, where the tradesman became a factory worker, owning neither the tools nor the raw materials of production.)

Throughout these years, cloth-makers from all over Europe sought English wool. Illustrative of the demand is a letter the Holy Roman Emperor Charlemagne sent to the English king Offa of Mercia around 850 C.E., requesting cloth made specifically from English wool.[2] Later, merchants commented that Spanish wool, though fine, was too short and required an admixture of longer English wool in order to make fine thread and thin cloth. Meanwhile, German and French wools were too coarse, making poor-quality cloth unless they too were mixed with English wool. During this era, it did not escape the English kings that they could use wool as a bargaining tool in their international business and political negotiations. Edward I exploited English wool to force alliances with the courts of Holland and Flanders. Later, in 1341, Edward III offered 583 wool sacks to the Flemish in exchange for support against the French in the Hundred Years' War.[3]

Wool trade with the Continent was so brisk throughout the tumultuous years of Saxon rule that by the time of the Norman Conquest in 1066, England's most important export product was wool. As trade grew, so did the role of merchants and middlemen in facilitating the production and transporting of wool from sheep-grower to cloth-maker. Increasingly, a middleman would buy the total annual wool crop from a large estate and then sell it to either another middleman, another market, or directly to other woolworkers, such as spinners and weavers. Sometimes the merchant would negotiate terms of sale with the wool producer at a defined marketplace, such as the annual wool fair; at other times, he would negotiate at the wool-grower's estate.

The expanding wool trade of the 13th and 14th centuries required new financing skills and tools. In the process, merchants established the fundamentals of modern capitalism, banking, and finance. Some of the most active wool traders in this era came from Italy in the form of papal agents who collected Church taxes.[4] At that time, when a local monastery could not provide ecclesiastical taxes in cash, they paid in sacks of wool. This transaction converted the tax collector into a wool merchant, because monetizing the wool required him to enter the wool market. In some situations, if the merchant desired to buy all the wool from a specific farm or region, he drew up futures contracts extending over a period between two and twenty years. These contracts at once assured the monasteries of an agreed-upon selling price for the wool they produced and guaranteed the merchants a set quantity and quality of wool for purchase at a certain date and price. Although these contracts served as insurance, they also posed risk. In some years, when a wool crop was poor, monasteries had to borrow money to pay the merchant; in other years, merchants could incur devastating losses if they were unable to sell the delivered wool at the negotiated price. After England separated from the Catholic Church in the mid-16th century, merchants changed from tax collectors to independent wool trader specialists.

Eventually, financing even a small part of the large wool market grew far beyond the ability of any one trader. The market encompassed multiple steps and each step involved its own risk: negotiating terms of wool purchase; assuring steady flow of raw materials to cloth manufacturing centers; underwriting the cost of weaving, fulling, and dyeing; and arranging delivery of finished cloth to the cloth markets. Ambitious merchants took on these trade risks in return for large profits. In the process, they became merchant bankers, controlling large amounts of capital, and employing both directly and indirectly thousands of people all over Europe. Merchant banking firms and families formed and from them arose the first large banking systems of Europe. In time, these banks accumulated enough wealth to support sovereigns and governmental projects.[5]

One of the most distinctive merchant-banker families in this era was the Medici. As early as 1297, the Medici family was a member of the Florentine wool-maker's guild, Arte della Lana. Although we don't know if they or their agents were negotiating in England, we do know this bank, Baco Medici, was founded on wealth from the wool trade and that Florence imported large quantities of English wool. From their vastly successful bank, the family acquired legendary wealth, which enabled them to influence, if not dominate, the politics of Florence and Rome of the time and to support great artists, including the sculptor and painter Michelangelo.

Another notable figure of this period who reaped benefits from the trade was Christopher Columbus. His father, Domenico, and the immediate family of his mother were all cloth-weavers. As late as 1472 in Savona, a town near Genoa, Columbus and his father were engaged in the wool trade. By 1473, Columbus had saved enough to invest in a local woolen company, and many of his seagoing opportunities were allegedly sponsored by proceeds from the Spanish wool trade.

For years, raw wool was England's primary export product, and its chief importers were the two major wool-processing centers of Europe: Flanders (roughly northern Belgium today) and Florence. Of the two, Flanders formed the larger market. One aspect of the trade that particularly piqued English sensitivity was its circular nature: The Flemish bought English wool, wove it into the finest cloth in Europe, and then sold it back to the English. Even though England raised the best wool, when it came to making cloth, their weavers couldn't compete.

In 1258, the rebellious Oxford Parliament—a breakaway Parliament consisting of noblemen resisting the policies of King Henry III—decreed that England must have its own high-quality wool cloth industry. So Parliament passed laws intended to promote the development of domestic cloth production. The laws restricted both cloth imports (mostly from Flanders) and raw wool exports (mostly to Flanders). Except for irritating the Flemish and manipulating the price of wool on the European market, these programs had little effect on the domestic wool industry. The king finally decided that England should entice the excellent Flemish weavers to England. But how?

Luckily, the English didn't have to do much to persuade the skilled Flemish weaver to decamp from Flanders, since harsh political and religious extremism in the Low Countries was sufficient motivation. Large numbers of Flemish cloth workers immigrated to England in two periods: first during the reign of Edward III in the 14th century and then during the reign of Elizabeth I in the 16th century. They quickly integrated themselves into the English work force and produced high-quality cloth, but more important, they taught the English how to produce fine cloth. By the second half of the 14th century, English broadcloth production had multiplied threefold, and its export multiplied even more: no less than ninefold. By the 16th century, England surpassed Flanders in the manufacture of woolens; one hundred years after that, fine woolen cloth comprised two-thirds of England's total exports.[6]

Not only did England now produce the best wool in the European world, it also wove the best woolen cloth. Despite these successes, the crown was downright jittery over the threat of competition. The government argued that since the wool trade was pivotal to the health of the British Empire, it needed protection. To that end, Parliament imposed an embargo on raw wool exports, forbade emigration of skilled woolworkers, restricted trade of raw wool by the American colonies, and campaigned for citizens to wear native, rather than foreign, textiles. Another jingoistic program was the "Burial in Woollen Acts" of 1666, mandating that Englishmen be buried in none other than pure English woolen shrouds at the risk of a fine.[7]

The wool trade brought fabled wealth to England during this period, benefitting every aspect of the economy: transportation, exploration, farming, industry, education, and religion. And throughout history, prominent British politicians have praised the contributions of wool to the glory of kingdom: In 1297, the barons of Parliament deemed it "the jewel of the realm"; Sir Francis Bacon called it "this great wheel" of the realm; King James II declared it to be "the greatest and most profitable commodity of this kingdom"[8]; and 15th-century wool merchant John Barton of Holme had a stamp in the window of his home proclaiming, "I thank God and ever shall, It is the sheep hath payed for all."[9]

Lest lawmakers forget what was buttering their bread, in the early part of the 14th century, Edward III ordered that sacks of wool be placed in the House of Lords "to put our judges in the House of Lords ever in mind of preserving and advancing the trade and manufacture of wool"—a tangible reminder of the significance of wool to English wealth. Even to this day, in a nod to wool's central role in British history, one of these sacks from the 14th century (though it's since been repacked with wool and repaired over the years) still sits on a chair in the center of the House of Lords opposite the throne.[10]

England's wool wealth was used for sundry purposes. In 1192, King Richard the Lionhearted, hero of the Robin Hood legend, was in trouble. On his journey home from the Holy Land and the Third Crusade, Richard—a prepossessing fellow who relished good battles, built imposing castles, and eschewed royal heir production—fell prisoner to the Duke of Austria. Eventually, the duke handed his captive over to Henry VI, the Holy Roman Emperor, who put Richard up for ransom. The emperor demanded 150,000 marks (equal to about $3 million today), a sum two to three times the annual income of the English crown at that time. Since England wanted Richard back, in 1194, the government appropriated the annual wool production—fifty thousand sacks—from two Cistercian abbeys and sold it on the wool market to generate the demanded funds.[11]

Almost a century and a half later, King Edward III used wool monies to finance his armies for the Hundred Years' War. From 1337 to 1453, the kingdoms of England and France were locked in a brutal battle over ownership of lands on the Continent (the English kings contended that the regions of France their forefathers possessed generations before still rightfully belonged to them). Edward took funds from wherever he could to support his campaigns, and since the wool market was the "cash cow" of the era, Edward made the most of it, imposing taxes on wool and borrowing money liberally from wool merchant-bankers.

The wool merchants certainly had money to spare, and when they weren't giving it to Edward, they were spending it abundantly themselves. Many of the rich cloth merchants became philanthropists and gave back to the country and the Church as an act of thanksgiving and celebration. Some chose to build churches in a demonstration of gratitude for their bountiful success. The resulting "Wool Churches," named in deference to the wellspring of the funds, still reside in the wool-growing regions of the Cotswolds and East Anglia.

One such church was made by wool merchant Michael de la Pole, Earl of Suffolk, who rebuilt St. Agnes's Church in the small village of Cawson, Norfolk, in the early 15th century, converting a small, simple chapel into a richly decorated church. Constructed of select French stone, the church tower stands tall at 120 feet. Inside, carvings of angels decorate the wooden hammer-beam nave ceiling, and outside, carvings of gargoyles decorate the portals. Sculpted within the portal frieze is the de la Pole family coat of arms. John Fortey, another successful wool merchant, bequeathed in his will of 1458 sums to the Cathedral of the Cotswolds (North-leach Church) to rebuild that church.[12] As a benefactor, he also contributed a brass etching of himself as an armored knight, one foot on a sheep and the other on a sack of wool. At the same time as Fortey was bankrolling this project, another wool merchant, Taddeo Taddei, commissioned Michelangelo for a sculpture, *Madonna and Child*, which now sits in the Royal Academy of Arts in London.

With so much emphasis on the well-to-do wool merchants, it's easy to forget that wool production actually begins with the person tending sheep: the shepherd, whose life was not easy then, nor is it today.[13] Day and night, shepherds grazed their herds on meadows and hillsides, ensuring that the sheep were properly fed, protected from predators, and growing quality wool, as well as successfully breeding and lambing. No matter where they worked, shepherds endured long hours, harsh weather, few benefits, and low pay. The pay generally consisted of a bowl of whey each day, whole milk on Sunday, one lamb at weaning time, one fleece at shearing time, the privilege of keeping his own sheep among the lord's flock, and the opportunity to bring his employer's sheep to his own agriculture plot for a fortnight of manuring.[14]

Shearing, the culmination of the year's husbandry and toil, took place in springtime. In contrast to the usual solitary, quiet, and slow pace of herding, wool harvesting was a time of bustle and coming together. In fact, many communities had a formal celebration, as with the sheep-shearing feast described by Shakespeare in Act IV of *The Winter's Tale*, when an abundance of holiday foods such as sugar, currants, rice, saffron, warden pies, mace, dates, ginger, prunes, raisins, hot lavender, mints, and savory marjoram were enjoyed along with music, dancing, and song.

But the party aside, there was serious work to be done with shearing. The shearer's challenge was to clip the fleece off without nipping the skin—a difficult process made that much harder by a sheep unwilling to stay still. The shearer would place the sheep on its rear end with its back against the operator's legs and its face pointing away. In this position, the sheep remains surprisingly quiet and docile during the clip. The shearer would use a double triangular iron blade cutter with a U-shaped spring that looked like a giant pair of rudimentary scissors and start at the neck, progressing downward over the belly, continuing upward from the hip to the nape of the neck, and finally finishing around the back. The shearer would try to cut the wool as close as possible to the skin in order to maximize fiber length. Because wool fibers bind to one another, the fleece comes off the sheep as a mat weighing from six to twenty-five pounds. Using the hand clipper, a shearer could remove a complete fleece in about five minutes; using electric clippers, the clip takes about one minute. Today, some farms actually collect fleece without using any shears at all by injecting a protein growth factor into the sheep's skin. This factor causes the hair to fracture in the deep follicle, allowing the fleece to peel off without scissors or clippers—a very high-tech approach.[15]

Woolworkers refer to all the fibers clipped from one sheep as "fleece," but the fleece actually contains different grades of fibers, all of which are used for different purposes. There are two main types of fibers in the fleece: "soft wool" (the thin, soft, curly fibers comprising the underfur of the fleece) and "hair wool" (the long, thick, rigid, straight fibers comprising the overfur of fleece).[16] The character of the individual wool fibers within fleece varies from breed to breed. Although the first domesticated sheep in England produced hair-rich wool, centuries of selective mating led to breeds growing mostly fine-fibered wool. Breeds of sheep producing particularly fine, short-fibered wool were developed along the Scottish and Welsh borders and on the Yorkshire moors. The most famous of these was the Ryeland breed, named after their feed by the monks who husbanded them. Craftspeople used the Ryeland's short and fine-fibered fleece for making soft yarn, loosely woven cloth, and felt. So soft was this wool that Queen Elizabeth I ruled that only Ryeland wool could be used for her royal stockings. Sheep producing long, fine-fibered soft wool came mainly from breeds such as the Lincoln and Cotswold. This type of wool commanded the highest price of all, because long fibers can be spun into strong, thin threads, and thin threads make up the finest cloth.[17]

Once sheared, the fleece must go to a wool classer, who is in charge of grading the fleece and separating its wool into these different categories. The classers of earlier days would separate wool into one of three bins. In the first, he would place the fine (thinnest) fibers and label them "wool"; in a second, he would put the coarse (thickest) fibers and label them "hair"; and to the third, he would add fibers that were neither fine nor coarse and call them "mixed." The finest fibers would go to make soft cloth for shirts, dresses, and pants, while the coarse fibers would be used for tough, longer-lasting cloth meant for carpets and draperies. (One exception was the hair shirt, made of coarse fibers and worn by religious figures under their outer garments and against their skin, where the itchy, prickly fibers would serve as a constant reminder of their sins and worldly temptations. Charlemagne was allegedly buried in such a hair shirt, which he had worn and borne during his life.) Over the years, the grading system for wool has become much more discriminating, so today wool may be classified into anywhere from six to sixteen different grades.

Once the fleece is sold, its processing begins. The wool must first be cleaned of pasture remnants (the dirt, sand, burrs, sticks, and dung that come from grazing freely outdoors) and natural products produced by the sheep's body, namely lanolin (which comes from the sheep's oil glands), and a crusty, flaky material called suint (which comes from their sweat glands). The person responsible for this cleansing process is called the scourer, who places the sorted raw wool in warm, soapy water and gently stirs it to remove the dirt. After rinsing with water, the scourer dries the wool either outside on a hanger or indoors using a drying chamber and hot air. Finally, the scourer fluffs and loosens the wool by hand.

Next comes the carder, who makes sure that the wool fibers all lie in one direction, which is necessary in order to create strong yarn or thread. To orient the fibers, the carder places the cleansed wool on a tablet covered by a regular array of rigid needles. This tablet is called a "card" because the ancient Romans combed and disentangled their wool using the dried, spiny fruit of the teasel plant, a plant they referred to as *carduus*.[18] Although wool factory workers used actual teasel fruits as late as the early 20th century, workers card today using either teasel-inspired hand cards or machines engineered with needlelike projections. When using the hand card, a worker places a clump of wool onto the surface of one card and then transfers it to a second card by brushing. The process is like brushing long hair; after enough strokes, the knots and tangles come out and the hairs lie straight. In the carding process, then, a clump of wool passes back and forth from one hand card to the other until the wool is free of knots and the fibers are aligned into a weblike wool mesh called a "batt." Next, the worker removes the batt from the card, gently rolls it up, and passes it on to the spinner.

The goal of spinning is to turn the aligned wool fibers into thread. The spinner places the carded wool on a stick called a distaff. The loaded distaff looks something like cotton candy on a cone, where the billowy wool takes the place of the candy. The spinner pulls wool off the distaff and twists it between thumb and first finger to form a thread. The spinner then lengthens the thread by pulling it and winding the formed end about a second stick, the spindle. On the end of the spindle is a round, flat stone or a clay ring, which acts as a flywheel, twisting and tightening the strands of wool as they are pulled off the distaff. Traditionally, the spinner stood up and fed wool onto the growing thread by pulling stock wool from the distaff, forming thread with the fingers, and dropping it to twist with the spinning spindle. When the spindle touched the floor, she would stop, wind up the thread on the bottom of the spindle, and start the process all over again. The spinner had to stand up because the farther she was from the floor, the longer the thread would be before she had to wind it up. Then, in the 14th century, the spinning wheel finally came to England. Using this new machine allowed the spinner to sit, because the spinning process was now horizontal. Nevertheless, spinning was still a very slow process; in fact, up until the 18th century, one productive weaver required the output of three to five spinners[19] in order to keep busy. Because spinning was such a painfully slow step in the wool-to-cloth process, the production of cloth could only increase when spinning at last became mechanized in the late 18th century. With the thread made, the next step is weaving it into cloth.

While the weaving tools used today are larger and faster than those used three thousand years ago, the principles are the same.[20] All weaving involves two perpendicularly positioned threads: one running up and down—the warp fibers—and the other interlacing in a right-to-left or left-to-right direction—the weft fibers.[21] Primitive European weavers used a vertical, warp-weighted loom; the weaver stood and the vertical warp fibers were weighted by stones or by a wooden beam. Then, in about 1000 c.e., the horizontal loom came to Europe. On this loom, threads lay parallel to the ground, with the warp threads projecting away from the weaver and the weft threads passing horizontally. The most revolutionary feature of the horizontal loom is that the weaver could sit down and weave for extended periods. During the time of the vertical loom, weavers—at least in Europe—were predominately (if not entirely) female. When the loom became horizontal, men replaced women in the job.[22] History books don't explain why the roles reversed, but now men were able to sit at looms, plying their skills and generating a significant income. In any event, once weaving developed into a trade, it moved out of the home into the marketplace—where men negotiated with men.

During the late 18th century, the wool trade met its first significant competitor, cotton, and then, two hundred years later, synthetic fibers. Because of these substitutes, the demand for wool and its production has steadily declined. In 2013, the global need for wool was one thirtieth of cotton and one seventieth of synthetic fiber.[23] Nevertheless, even though wool no longer dominates the cloth market, its production and use are still significant. For example, in 2014, the world's wool production reached 4.6 billion pounds, with Australia, New Zealand, and China producing the most (45 percent of the total)[24] and China consuming the most (60 percent of world production).

Compared to other fibrous materials, wool—like all hair—has uniquely useful properties, particularly with regard to its ability to absorb sweat, retain heat, resist electrical current or fire, and stretch. But when it comes to shrinking (a negative quality of wool cloth, largely because of the wool fiber cuticle), other fibers like cottons and polyesters are more attractive. The wool industry has responded to this disadvantage by treating wool fibers so that they shrink much less. However, there is another disadvantage to wool: the fact that it is less "green" than other materials used for cloth. Compared to the production of silk, cotton, and polypropylene, wool—from the tending of sheep to the dyeing of cloth—is more environmentally expensive. Today, there are about one billion sheep grazing the earth, with each sheep foraging about twenty-five pounds of pasturage each day and emitting large quantities of digestive gases (worldwide, livestock contributes about 20 percent of all emitted greenhouse gases).[25] In addition, wool cleansing and dyeing require copious amounts of water: about a hundred gallons to make one pound of wool.[26] Because it is so environmentally unfriendly to produce, the other fiber substitutes are again much more attractive. While it is hard to envision a world without wool clothes, the current trend is certainly moving toward a world with fewer.

13

BEYOND CLOTHES

—

*The first tennis balls were elastic because of the hair
packed in their center.*

Well before they wove it into cloth, primitive people used
natural fibers in their daily life. Out of fibers, they made
ropes, baskets, nets, weirs, cages, weapons, and musical
instruments. They collected plant fibers from tree stems, grasses,
flax, and jute, and they collected animal fibers from hair, silk, skin,
and gut. Arguably, the most useful of these fibers is hair because of
its accessibility and properties. While the first application for hair
was structural, that is, as a thread, it gradually became a tool for

health researchers, criminologists, and industrialists who learned that hair is a repository of useful chemicals as well. Some of these chemicals reveal secrets about the person or animal producing it and others contribute to industrial needs. Aside from cloth, the uses of hair are widespread and numerous, showing up in places you would least expect.

Hair has played an important role in the visual arts, because artists need brushes, and brushes are made of hair. All brushes, whatever the use—artistic, house painting, pastry—share the same basic makeup: namely a grip or handle, a bristle or head, and a ferrule, which is a waist-belt holding the two ends together. The workhorse of the brush is called the bristle because the earliest brushes were made of pig hairs of the same name. Hair fibers are glued into the brush ferrule with all hair shafts oriented so that the tips point toward the brush tip. This placement certifies that the working end of the brush has a very fine delivery point and the cuticle orientation is the same for all fibers.

The kind of hair making up the bristle dictates what can be done with a given paintbrush. Coarse and stiff porcine hairs are best for broad strokes but not for detail. Thin, soft, supple hairs such as those from sable, squirrel tail, badger, polecat, horse (from which belly, ears, mane, and tail all provide the right fiber), and cow's ear are best for detail. Among fine artists, the choicest bristles come from the underside of the tail of a male Siberian sable during winter. This hair is prized not only for its length (as long as two and a half inches) but also for its needle-sharp tips, prominent cuticle, and structural resiliency. These brushes hold a flame-shaped bristle with a very narrow tip and a swollen belly. The bristle hairs and their prominent cuticles wick up and hold the paint, allowing the artist to draw a long, thin line. During the process of applying paint, the flamelike shape of the bristle flattens, the hairs flare, and the fine tip breaks up. Because of its unique elasticity, a sable hair bristle will regain its useful shape and sharp tip merely by a gentle flick.

But sable-haired brushes are not cheap. Manufacturers obtain the hairs by plucking or shaving the tails of slaughtered animals and, as it takes about three hundred tails to give one pound of hair, it is no surprise that a large sable brush can cost more than $1,000. As a result, artists are demanding better, cheaper synthetic-bristled brushes. While modern synthetic fibers may be as elastic as hair, they don't hold their shape as well and, lacking a cuticle, they don't hold paint as well. (Synthetic brushes are just fine for basic uses, such as house painting; in fact, they make up 80 percent of the paintbrushes sold in the world market today.[1]) Ongoing industrial research promises that synthetic fibers in the future will better approximate the tapered tip and grooved or roughened surface of natural fibers.

Another kind of artist whose livelihood depends on hair is the musician. Although musicologists argue about the origin of the violin bow, most relate it to the pick, a small, flat piece of wood, metal, or plastic that guitar or mandolin players use to pluck or strum strings. Employing a bow to vibrate a musical string is like a very rapid series of plucks. The notion is that the successive catch-and-release of sticky bow hairs over a musical string imparts such rapid plucks that the resultant note is continuous and smooth.

The bow of a string instrument, such as a violin, viola, or cello, consists of a wooden stick or rod with head and grip ends. Stretching between the head and the grip is a hank of hair. The grip contains a screw mechanism that allows the player to increase or reduce bow-hair tension. As with the paintbrush, the best bow hair comes from a very special host: the tail of a white Siberian or Mongolian stallion. These breeds are choice because animals living in a cold climate grow stronger hair; males are preferred because their tail hairs are not routinely exposed to urine. (Urine is injurious to hair because it softens hair shafts and causes the cuticle cells to flare open.)

Bow hair arrives from the importer as a three-foot-long hank of clean, white shafts weighing one to two pounds. When stringing a bow, the bow-maker, or archetier, uses about 130 to 150 straight, non-curled shafts. She ties a thread around the head end of the hank, secures the tie with melted rosin and inserts the tied end into the head end of the bow. Next, she combs the hairs to make sure none are overlapping, and then she ties the other end of the hank and seals it with melted rosin. Finally, she moistens the hank so that the shafts soften and then she inserts it into the grip. As the hairs dry, they become taut; the degree of tension is later adjusted using the screw mechanism on the grip. It generally takes an apprentice about six months to learn how to rehair a bow and about three years to learn how to make one. A bow played regularly needs rehairing every six months.

Musicians in the percussion section also use hair in the form of wool-felt to cushion the contact between two surfaces. All percussion instruments use a variety of hammers to elicit sounds from an intact surface or string. In some instances, the music calls for a hard, crisp *click* and in other instances a dull, soft *puff*. For hard sounds, the hammers are naked, made of wood or metal; for soft sounds, they are wrapped in felt or soft wool. Musicians use felt-wrapped hammers on band parade drums, side drums, snare drums, tympani, xylophones, tubular bells, and Chinese gongs. Felt dampens instrument contact because of the elastic properties of its constituent hairs.

The piano is another percussion instrument requiring cushioning. Pressing a piano key causes a wool-felt-padded hammer to strike steel strings; then, when the key is released, a felt-lined damper stops the string's vibration and thus the sound. But all keys are not covered by the same type of felt, because felt stiffness influences the musical pitch. Felt comes in a wide spectrum of densities depending on how much heat and pressure are brought to bear on the starting wool. Hammers covered with hard felt deliver high notes and those covered with soft felt give low notes. In this sense, between the pianist and his music there is always a hairy layer.

Sportsmen also use hair—perhaps surprisingly, in fishing. In mid-17th-century London, Izaak Walton and Charles Cotton, two wealthy businessmen, wrote a book called *The Compleat Angler*[2] describing everything they knew about their favorite hobby: fly fishing. Written for the amateur, the book describes in detail how to catch fish and how to cook them. (The book is worth a read today, not only for the details of angling but also for the dialogue, which is rich with descriptions of life experiences, history, literature, legend, and philosophy.) Walton and Cotton also considered hair the best fishing tackle (line) because of its strength, light weight, and variable color. But not all hairs are equally endowed. They advise the fisherman to "take care that [the hairs used for tackle] be round and clear, free of galls." For them, the ideal tackle line hair was round (which meant it was strong) and of "glass-colour," so that it was barely visible in water. And for them, the best hair came from white horse tails. Though hair still decorates lures today, amateur and professional fishermen now use tackle made of synthetic materials.

Hair also surfaces in the history of tennis. The original tennis ball, as standardized by King Louis XI in 1480, consisted of a leather cover with tightly packed hair or wool inside. By the 18th century, organized strips of felted wool replaced the leather covering but the center still consisted of densely packed hair or wool. But why hair? To serve its bouncing function, the tennis ball had to be made of the most elastic material available at the time, and that material was hair, so it was reasonable to pack wool or hair into a ball that had to bounce.[3] Modern tennis balls get a more substantial bounce from their rubber mantle and air-filled center but the hair is still there in the form of its felted wool cover.[4]

Hair's use has not been limited to recreational purposes; it has also played a role in cleaning up environmental catastrophes. In March of 1989, the *Exxon Valdez* ran aground in Alaska, spilling ten million gallons of oil into Prince William Sound. The media broadcasted photographs of oil-covered sea otters and sea fowl, revealing a major wildlife tragedy. Most people simply shook their heads in despair. But Phil McCrury, a hairdresser in Madison, Alabama, saw an opportunity. McCrury posited that as hair is normally covered with oils from the sebaceous glands, it must have an inherent property to take up oil. He concluded that hair should be an efficient means for removing oil from water. The oil-soaked animals were already proving that. If otter hair could pick up oil, then human hair should work as well; after all, hair is hair. To test this notion, McCrury collected untreated human hair from his salon, stuffed it into pantyhose, and placed the hair–pantyhose pillow into a concoction of motor oil and water. In the space of a few minutes, the pillow had taken up the oil and cleaned the water. Inspired by McCrury's observation, Lisa Gautier, an environmentalist, set about making hair blankets that could be used in the case of an oil spill. In November 2007, when a Korean tanker crashed into the San Francisco Bay Bridge and emptied more than 53,000 pounds of oil into the Bay, Gautier and other volunteers were able to use the hair blankets to assist with the cleanup.[5, 6]

Hair may be able to wipe away oil, but its ability to retain secrets is what makes it so useful in forensics. Just as the experienced forensic investigator can use fingerprints as evidence in a crime, so too can hair lead to insight. Edgar Allan Poe illustrated this point in a short story, "The Murders in the Rue Morgue," in which two women in an upper-level apartment are viciously murdered. The investigators are confounded by the superhuman violence of the crime and the fact that the murderer could only have gained entrance by means of a drainpipe adjacent to a living room window. When one of the detectives finds and examines short red hairs between the clutching fingers of one of the murdered women, he proclaims, "This is no human hair!" Realizing the culprit must be an animal, the police seek and eventually find an agitated orangutan in possession of a shaving razor rampaging the streets of Paris. As this story illustrates, an unattached hair can reveal something about the animal or person who grew it.

Hair is used to provide valuable forensic evidence for several reasons. First, in a criminal investigation, hair may be the only physical evidence available, since both victim and villain shed hairs continuously. A person normally loses from ten to a hundred scalp hairs each day; in addition, people lose hair from the underarms, beard, body, and groin. Second, hair is easy to obtain from suspects for testing because it is expendable and can be donated, repeatedly if necessary, without threatening privacy or causing tissue injury to the donor. Third, hair is stable compared to blood, urine, or soft body tissues. The chemicals of a dry hair fiber may last for centuries. Finally, a single hair alone can yield information regarding the who, the what, and the when of a crime.

When the investigator finds hair at the crime scene, he or she must first record where it was found—in the victim's hand, on the victim's underpants, on the adjacent rug, on the butler's glove, or on the wainscoting. Of course, a discovered hair does not necessarily denote relevance: People and pets living in the area may have shed plenty of hair in the scene beforehand and, further, since hairs stick to other hairs (such as the hairs making up clothes), they can readily be transferred from place to place. Though hair shape similarities or differences can serve to include or exclude human suspects, shape alone cannot positively identify a suspect. The investigator must remember first that many different types of hair grow on one's body; short, long, thin, thick, wavy, curled, light, and dark hairs can all come from a single person. Second, certain racial groups have predominately one type of hair, but no one hair type is limited to one racial group: Straight hairs grow on African people and tight, curly hair on Indo-Europeans and Asians. The inclusion-exclusion decision depends on a side-by-side comparison of hairs found on the victim, hairs taken from the victim, and hairs taken from the suspect. And only extreme differences in hair type are meaningful. For example, if the suspicious hair found adjacent to the victim is straight and light and the accused has tightly curled black hair, it is reasonable to exclude this suspect; however, if the hair adjacent to the victim is tightly curled and black, it would be just as reasonable not to exclude this subject.

Despite the limitations of hair shape in crime resolution, prosecutors have presented hair as evidence and juries have uncritically accepted that evidence with tragic consequences. Recently, the Federal Bureau of Investigation acknowledged that between 1985 and 1999, experts in their laboratories used hair shape and color evidence in at least twenty-one hundred cases to positively identify suspects[7] and that some of these judgments were based on incomplete or misleading statistics. One such case was that of Donald Gates, who was accused of the murder and rape of a 21-year-old college student found naked and dead in June 1981 in Rock Creek Park, in Washington, D.C. There were two major points against him presented at trial. The first was testimony from a police informant who reported that he witnessed Gates killing the victim. What the jury did not know was that the informant was also a felon and that the police had offered to reduce his charges and pay him for his testimony. Second was the damning laboratory evidence supplied by an FBI forensic agent who had recklessly concluded that the foreign hairs on the victim's body were microscopically indistinguishable from Gates's body hair.[8] As it turned out, those hairs did not belong to Gates and, after twenty-eight years in prison, Gates was exonerated by means of DNA analysis, which showed that semen on the victim's body could not have come from Gates. This goes to show that while hair can often serve as an accurate reflection of the body from which it arises, it is far from perfect evidence. The challenge for the forensic investigator is to make absolutely certain the hairs used for analysis—and subsequently for trial evidence—are relevant to the case and have not been contaminated by other unrelated environmental agents (sweat, dirt, bugs, etc.). Until such a time when the outside elements can be confidently separated from the hair itself, hair shape must be used as a piece of supporting evidence, but it cannot be the sole incriminating evidence.

The chemistry of hair, however, doesn't lie, as was shown in a case that arose in Middlesex County, New Jersey, in 2013.[9] Pharmaceutical chemist Tinale Li had had frequent disputes with her husband, which on sixteen occasions required police intervention at their suburban home. Then, one day, he turned up dead—and Li was the prime suspect. But how did she do it? A toxicology expert found thallium—a perfect poison: tasteless, odorless, and lethal—in body fluids including the hair shafts taken from the deceased. It turned out that Li had access to the drug at the pharmaceutical company where she worked; company records indicated that she had used some of it without documentation.[10] Though her attorney argued she was innocent, the hair evidence was compelling, and the jury found Li guilty of murder.

Another record provided by hair is genetic. Since hair shafts are made of fossilized body cells, they contain all the important molecules of life, including deoxyribonucleic acid, or DNA, a chainlike molecule made of four different chemical links (adenine, thymine, guanine, and cytosine). Because the order of the links varies from person to person, individual people can be distinguished and identified by the DNA found in hair shafts, almost like a fingerprint.[11] Although DNA from hair is used in criminal cases today with caution because of the ever challenging issue of provenance, historians have used it to validate records. One example concerns the French Revolution and the royal family. History makes clear that both King Louis XVI and his queen, Marie Antoinette, died on the guillotine, but the documents do not unequivocally describe what happened to their ten-year-old son, the Dauphine, who by tradition should have become King Louis XVII. It was alleged that the young king was confined to the dungeon of the Temple prison and died of tuberculosis there two years later. It is also believed that, during the autopsy, the physician to the young king surreptitiously stole the child's heart, which passed through several hands until it eventually ended up as a relic in the basilica of St. Denis. The official story is that, since the king died so young, he died without an heir. But almost since the time of the revolution, there had been a series of rumors claiming that the young king actually escaped the dungeon and lived to sire an heir. In order to test the story, historian-scientists compared the sequence of DNA from the relic heart along with DNA collected from hair in jewelry lockets belonging to Marie Antoinette and her two sisters. The analysis confirmed that the child's heart came from a person who was related to the queen and that the child was most likely the young king.[12] Though the rumors may persist, the heart-hair-derived data are considered to be strong enough to dismiss any future claimant.

In addition to one's lineage, hair also records a history of one's own life. Just as film strips are made of a large number of single picture frames, each showing a very short episode in the larger story, so it is with the formation of the hair shaft. Each day, cells add to the shaft base and the shaft moves up a notch, with that cell containing a description of the health of its owner on that very day. Hair follicle cells will contain chemicals from the blood because the hair follicle is fed by small vessels surrounding its base. If a person had a portion of mercury-contaminated fish, for example, the mercury blood level would rise and some of the mercury would enter the cells incorporating into the bottom of all growing hair shafts. Since hair shafts grow out of the skin at a rate of a half inch per month, three months after the meal, a mercury-labeled "frame" would appear about one inch above the skin surface. If the person had only one tainted fish dinner, the mercury content of the shaft above and below this "frame" would be zero. This kind of long-term chemical record housed in the hair shaft presents a potent investigative tool for forensic scientists

In drug-facilitated crimes, the perpetrator may strive to impose a brief period of amnesia or unconsciousness on his victims and during this time he rapes, robs, or subdues them. In the typical scenario, the predator surreptitiously spikes the drink of an unsuspecting person with a psychotropic drug, which may be a pharmaceutical, hypnotic, anesthetic, street drug, or, most commonly, alcohol. Although protocol demands that investigators conduct a laboratory analysis of both victim and accused in such cases, the forensic investigator often ends up with no evidence of drugs in any body fluid. This is because victims characteristically don't realize they've been abused until days, if not months, later. Tissues, urine, and blood become drug-free between six hours and five days following consumption, so the examiner must look to a more stable repository of drugs. That's where hair comes in. In 2007, a nineteen-year-old girl who believed she had been raped reported to police that she only remembered having had a soft drink at a social gathering, but woke up disheveled and almost certain she had been assaulted. One month after the alleged episode, forensic pathologist Pascal Kintz received cut hair from the claimant and found that the hair contained a high concentration of the drug ketamine, a sedative that causes confusion and amnesia, with the highest concentration about one inch above the skin surface. Considering the rate of hair growth, it was highly likely that the victim had been exposed to the drug about one month previously. When confronted with this data, the accused confessed.[13]

By the same approach, hair can be useful in detecting doping in sports such as cycling, running, and boxing or in resolving medical questions. Physicians trying to find out why a prescribed drug is not working may look for the medicine in the patient's hair in order to determine if the drug is inactive, not absorbed, or not taken by the patient at all. Hair taken from a newborn can also indicate if a mother had been using drugs during her pregnancy, allowing doctors to know how to treat the infant. Veterinarians, too, use hair to test if grazing animals have been exposed to contaminated soil.[14]

But when important decisions are based on the chemical content of hair, the investigator must be sure that the chemicals found are from the body and not from tonics, shampoos, conditioners, dyes, room dust, or other environmental factors.[15] When Swedish physician and amateur historian Sten Forshufvud reported in 1961 that multiple hairs taken from the corpse of Napoleon Bonaparte contained a high concentration of arsenic, history buffs sat up to listen. Up to that time, scholars had accepted that Napoleon died of stomach cancer. The arsenic finding sent a generation of historians into a tizzy. Who fed him arsenic? It could have been French Republicans, French Royalists, British Royalists, ambitious and malevolent attendants—anyone, really. Forshufvud's report indicated that arsenic was associated with Napoleon's hair, but it didn't show how it got there. Had it been added to his food? Was it in his medication? Did it come from coal dust, wood smoke, wallpaper glue particles, or embalming materials? Because recent repeat analyses of the emperor's hair showed a significant quantity of bromine, iron, mercury, potassium, and antimony in addition to arsenic,[16] investigators concluded the arsenic found in Napoleon's hair was more likely a component of his environment.

As the hair shaft is 93 percent protein, hair could make up a nourishing dinner if we could digest it. In fact components of hair do contribute to both animal and human feed. Industrial chemists have found that heat and pressure will break down feathers (also a keratin structure) and hair to soluble protein-rich chunks that can be used as animal food supplements. Currently, while hair is not widely used as a protein additive resource in the West, digested feathers are. Two percent of the protein fed to chickens in the poultry food industry comes from feathers[17]—but chickens are not the only animals to have feather- or hair-derived ingredients in their food.

The food industry uses cysteine as a food additive, and some of the cysteine used for human food comes from human hair.[18] Mixing cysteine with sugars generates chemical derivatives that give food the aroma of cooked meat and, depending on the sugar content, the flavor will resemble beef, chicken, or pork. These flavor enhancers are added to many processed foods. Also, bakers add cysteine to flour dough in order to soften it and make it more machine-workable. Cysteine acts by breaking disulfide bonds that hold the large gluten protein networks together; softening dough with cysteine allows for shorter mixing times, improved machinability, and increased loaf volume. For this purpose, duck feather–and–human hair-derived cysteine gets into cookies, pizza, tortillas, crackers, biscuits, breadsticks, hamburger buns, bagels, and baguettes. So components of hair do get into processed food: It's just one of the many ways that hair has a presence—though quite unexpected for most modern consumers—in human life.

A GLIMPSE OF THE FUTURE

"All things change except barbers, the ways of barbers,
and the surroundings of barbers."
—Mark Twain, "About Barbers"[1, 2]

T he barbershop Twain described at least a century ago is not too different from the one I frequent today. In fact, present-day shops appear to evoke that earlier era. First, unlike most downtown businesses, barbershops are still largely non-franchised, individually owned, and independently operated. Next, except for the anachronistic, incessantly blaring television, barbershop decor is usually traditional, with white tile floors, mirror-lined walls, mahogany cabinets, marble shelves, and throne–like swivel chairs. Third, the haircutting experience still includes comb, scissors, clipper, and when done, itchy hair bits down the back and hair clumps on the floor. But hair care itself has changed a great deal since that time and, with advancing science and research, promises to evolve in exciting ways.

Visionaries predict the haircutting experience will be more mechanical in the future. Consider that there is already on the market a device called Robocut that is designed for self-delivered haircuts. It trims hair without a traditional comb or scissors. The instrument consists of a fan that draws hair into a tube. At the end of the tube is a moving blade that cuts the trailing hair. Currently, the device is handheld and hand-operated. Robocut inventor Alfred Natrasevschi envisions that the device can and will be adapted to full robot-operated hair trimming in the future.[3] Using such a construct, a haircutting robot could be programmed to remember the head dimensions and desired style for each client and thus be able to deliver the same service to each client time after time. With some adaptation, one could envision that the haircutting robot would shampoo hair and scalp or even clean the hair alone without involving the scalp. Moreover, the robot could spray materials onto the flowing hair to strengthen, curl, straighten, or color shafts.

Although this technology is doable, there are hurdles. First, entrepreneurial barbers and engineers will have to demonstrate that robot trims are as good as the traditional ones. Second, clients will have to choose the new cutting experience over the conventional cut; and third, investors supporting this innovation will have to commit significant capital to cover start-up costs. Although robot prototype design and construction are pricey (ranging from $10 to $15 million), the cost for a single robot working in an individual shop will be significantly less. To successfully introduce this robot into salon–barbershops, initial investors will have to demonstrate the efficacy of robotic hair care: reproducibly acceptable haircuts as fast as a stylist at a comparable price.

But in addition to the technology of the haircut, ongoing basic research suggests that in the future we will have fundamentally new ways to influence hair growth. More than fifty years ago, New York City dermatologist and surgeon Norman Orentreich demonstrated that hair follicles transplanted from the side of the scalp to the bald spot on top of the scalp grew as if they were still on the side of the scalp.[4] This was an unexpected finding because it indicated that each follicle behaves independently of its neighboring follicles, something like a petunia growing in an onion patch. Using this method, Orentreich claimed that he could treat balding by transplanting healthy follicles from anywhere on the body to any bald area.[5] This observation launched the surgical specialty of hair transplantation, which, since then, has served as the cornerstone therapy for common balding.

During hair transplantation, the surgeon either removes a thin strip of scalp from the back of the client's head and then dissects out individual hair follicles, or uses a surgical punch and removes individual follicles. The surgeon then implants the isolated follicles, one by one, into the bald areas. During the procedure, the surgical team typically relocates about two thousand hair follicles from the back of the head to the top. Although the procedure is expensive—in the range of $6,000[6]—once the transplanted follicles start producing hair, the patient is "cured." The bald spot is now covered by hair and those hairs will continue to grow— forever. The procedure is safe and effective, and, in most cases, the result satisfactory, if not excellent.

Dr. Ken Washenik, the president of Bosley Medical Groups, a hair transplantation company, says that although 90 percent of balding men want to restore their hair, only 10 percent select the transplant option; most are deterred by the idea of surgery and its high cost. Still, demand is large—and growing. In 2014, about four hundred thousand patients were treated worldwide—almost twice the number in 2004.[7] Washenik predicts that as skilled medical assistants (in place of high-cost surgeons) and mechanical devices perform more of the process, transplantation costs will drop.

In fact, robots are already assisting surgeons during this long and tedious procedure. The current robot is able to identify and extract suitable hair follicles from the shaved scalp, excising one at a time. Because the robot eliminates the need for cutting out a piece of scalp skin, the new process involves less blood loss, no hair follicle dissection, and rapid recovery with minimal scarring. The robot knows where the donor follicles are, how to remove them, and where the new follicles should be implanted. Engineers believe that by 2020 the robot will also know how to place donor follicles into the skin and, as such, be able to execute the whole hair transplant procedure.[8] Because the current robot has been very well received, one can predict that, by mid-century, the robot-implemented procedure will be widely available and affordable.

The major limitation of hair transplantation, either by hand or robot, is that there is no increase in hair follicles. Follicles are taken from one site and implanted into another, a zero-sum operation. After three or more transplantation procedures, if the surgeon (or robot) continues to take follicles out of one donor site, the site will begin to look more and more like the bald spot itself. At this point, the patient and his surgeon become keenly interested in generating brand-new follicles; they look to the bioengineer for help.

A bioengineer is the scientist who drives the field of regenerative medicine, spending creative hours trying to form new body parts, organs, and tissues for people who have lost them, say, a leg for a veteran, a new kidney for a diabetes patient, or a heart valve for a child born without one. Regenerating any organ requires stem cells, and as we have seen, these cells have the unique ability to engender more stem cells, as well as cells that can reproduce the parent organ: Liver stem cells will generate liver and pancreatic islet stem cells insulin-producing islets. The hair follicle also has stem cells and, as we have seen, when these cells are isolated and combined with dermal papilla cells, they form new hair follicles.

So the bioengineer's job sounds simple: Take stem cells from hair follicles, combine them with dermal papilla cells, form follicle precursors, and finally send them back to the hair transplantation surgeon (or transplantation robot) for proper placement into the patient's scalp. Actually, in the research laboratory, scientists from all over the world have generated mature cycling hair follicles literally thousands of times, from mouse hair follicle cells. So the biology of making hair follicles from isolated cells is eminently possible. As far as the surgeon is concerned, though, this accomplishment is limited, first, because the studies were done using mouse cells, and second, because the cells were not expanded in tissue culture.

Regarding the first concern, bioengineers contend that if mouse cells can regenerate follicles, then so will human cells, though that claim must be tested. The second concern relates to the ability to grow many brand-new hair follicles. This means starting out with a few donor follicles and making thousands more in the laboratory. And the only way the bioengineer can do this is by growing hair follicle stem cells—millions of them—in tissue culture. Growing stem cells in culture is challenging because if the conditions are not just right, the cells forget they are stem cells; yet more, they forget they're hair follicle cells altogether. In fact, this is the principal challenge for present-day bioengineers: to ascertain what any stem cell requires in order to grow in culture.

Over the last several years, preliminary experiments suggest that human stem cells can grow in tissue culture and they will maintain their hair follicle–forming ability. Only after scientists reproduce this finding many times, however, will it be proper to go on to the next step, namely, to explore how to transfer the cells from the laboratory to the clinic and how to place them into the scalp. At the same time, we must demonstrate that the implanted stem cells make normal shaft-producing hair follicles every time and that the regeneration process is safe. These studies will set the stage for cell-based therapies, and though such therapies will occur in the future hair care center, the science is not quite there yet. It will take several more decades before we get follicle regeneration from stem cells into the clinic, but there is no doubt it will come.

In 2012, the Nobel Prize in Physiology or Medicine was awarded to John Gurdon and Shinya Yamanaka for their work showing that one cell could be converted into another cell by a mix of very special chemicals. Yamanaka reported that inserting a combination of four special growth factors[9] into any cell switched that cell into a stem cell. This discovery was groundbreaking to bioengineers because it provided a method for them to generate any cell from any other—if they knew the proper chemical mix. This new approach enables bioengineers to reprogram a mature cell into a stem cell, a mature cell into another mature cell, or even a cancer cell back into a normal cell. Exploiting this approach, laboratories over the world are even now reporting spectacular successes: Consider the conversion of a gallbladder cell into a liver cell,[10] connective tissue cell into a heart muscle cell,[11] and skeletal muscle cell into a blood vessel cell.[12]

The research challenge for us is to find the proper mix of growth factors that will coax normal dermal cells into hair follicles wherever we want. Using this approach, we will not need to isolate, grow, or inject stem cells: The applied chemicals should do the job. Needless to add, scientists in a number of research laboratories are actively searching for the reprogramming chemicals. But how will we get the chemicals into the skin at the very site needing a hair follicle?

When you swallow an aspirin for a headache, it enters the blood and the blood distributes it to all organs and tissues of the body, including hair follicles; however, as far as the headache is concerned, aspirin works as an anodyne only when it reaches the vessels of the brain. This is not a very efficient use of aspirin and, clearly, not the way to deliver a hair follicle–inducing chemical. After all, we choose to have hair follicles only in certain skin regions, not all over the body. Our bioengineering goal, then, is to deliver such powerful transforming chemical cocktails only to the very spot we want hair. So our delivery must be very specific, and one of the most promising ways we can achieve such bull's-eye delivery is by means of nanoparticles: very small spherical chemical packages in the range of a millionth of an inch wide, which are able to carry and deliver materials. Because they are so small, nanoparticles are able to deposit their cargo into any biological cell or organ. The way a nanoparticle spreads in the body depends on its surface. If its surface is made of lipids (fats), it will home to areas of lipid, such as cell membranes. If its surface is negatively charged, it will home to positively charged surfaces. If its surface bears androgen molecules, it will stick to cells with androgen receptors. Because they can be manufactured to home to a very specific address (such as an androgen receptor), we envision that we could use such intelligent particles to deliver hair follicle–forming chemicals to cells—once we know the important chemical cocktails. The nanoparticle promises to be the delivery package, but we still need to know more about the biology.

The hair care salon will also address unwanted hair. Some clients want to get rid of their hair permanently, once and forever.

Irreversibly removing hair is not an easy chore because the follicle has robust regenerative properties; it takes a lot of punishment to both its epidermal and surrounding dermal structure in order to kill it. Today, cosmeticians use electrolysis and lasers to do the job. Electrolysis burns and destroys follicles of any size or color, because the process depends on delivering heat to the whole follicle and its surroundings. Laser hair removal is more selective, easier to apply, and less painful because the energy delivered is taken up only by the pigmented portions of the lower hair follicle. Laser treatments are considered so safe today that the process is often self-administered.

Other clients may want to keep their options open by only temporarily removing hair. This choice is more challenging. Today, if you want to remove your hair but keep its follicle, you either shave or treat the shafts with depilatory creams, which are chemicals that dissolve hair. But there must be a better solution. As we mentioned earlier, negative growth factors control hair follicle formation and cycling. The new notion would be to temporarily block hair growth by applying onto the skin the same negative growth factors that normally keep a hair follicle in telogen, the resting phase of the hair cycle. But if we are to benefit from this physiological approach in the next several decades, we will have to first answer some questions: Which factor or combination of factors must we use? At what concentration? And how do we give it? While these questions are unanswered today, there is no doubt this approach is doable and will come to hair care in this century.

Futurists also envision that the new barbershop will offer much more than our traditional barbering or salon experience; it will embrace the facilities of an all-around cosmetic center. It will be a one-stop, "holistic" beauty-care community for men and women of all hair types, reminiscent of a food court with multiple stations in a large, easily accessible area. The center will be highly mechanized with full database support and robotic assistance. Not only will there be exercise and nutrition coaches, but there will also be tattoo health services, eye- and nail-care stations, and dermatological facilities, in addition to a wig station with computer-assisted wig weaving, fitting, and repair. Furthermore, there will be hair removal stations (with support for both permanent and transient hair-growth cessation), hair transplant stations with robot assistance, and hair growth stations, with cell-based and off-the-shelf growth factor–based applications. In the center, highly trained estheticians will oversee and execute most of the cosmetic procedures surgeons handle today. It's an exciting future that, interestingly enough, may look oddly reminiscent of the barber-surgeons of days past. Above all, if the technological and scientific advances in this century are as great as they were in the last, our projections here will have been much too humble.

Hair has played a major role in human history, and far into the future this remarkable fiber will continue to weave its way into the story of our lives. I am certain its tale will be part of our first conversation with those extraterrestrial life-forms who want to know more about our fuzzy exterior—though I would be surprised if they too did not have their own sort of hair, with very similar properties and messages.

ACKNOWLEDGMENTS

—

Writing a book is like embarking on a long-wanted voyage. There are stages in the making. Deciding on the trip. Collecting information. Making travel plans. Suffering the vicissitudes of getting there. Once there, sorting out what is worthwhile, what is necessary, and what is expendable. Finally, recognizing and appreciating the many people along the way—from bus driver to tour leader to croissant baker—who made the experience possible and worthwhile.

This trip could not have been made without the help of many people who generously provided encouragement, ideas, criticisms, and materials. Tom George first suggested the idea for this book during a festive Christmas dinner at the Institute of Advanced Studies, though the launch waited for my barber's probing question. As I started out, the late Bill Beller, a successful nonfiction writer, helped me with the mechanics of writing a trade book. Throughout the writing, I have had the resources of several outstanding libraries and their staff: the University of Pennsylvania, Princeton University,

Drexel University, Georgia Institute of Technology, Princeton Public Library, and the National Library of Scotland. Several colleagues I called upon over and over again for their help and insight: Professor Anonda Bell, Professor George Cotsarelis, Alan Herscovici, Professor Ralf Paus, Professor George Rogers, Linda Rossin, and Dr. Ken Washenik. For ideas and assistance on specific topics, I am grateful to Leila Cohoon, Rebecca Esmi, Julie Gerow, Adam Green, Mike Ippoliti, Charles Kirkpatrick, Yves LeFur, Richard Mawbey, Andrea Stryer, Katya Svoboda, and to Professors Rox Anderson, Petra Arck, Judy Brodsky, Cheng Ming Chuong, Elaine Fuchs, Colin Jahoda, Paradi Mirmirani, Roy Oliver, Jerry Shapiro, Desmond Tobin, and Annika Vogt. I am indebted to Professor Vera Price for her advice and friendship over many years. Despite all of this unparalleled and valuable counsel, I alone have had to make the hard choices and so the mistakes inherent are mine.

I was very fortunate during this journey to have had an incisive, dedicated, and rigorous literary agent, Regina Ryan, who demanded the best and patiently pointed out what it takes. In the process of composing the proposal, Abigail Wilentz gently and perceptively suggested lucid writing and rhetorical solutions. I have had the unique fortune of a literary editor at Pegasus, Iris Blasi, who not only understood my vision but worked closely with me in the final writing process to make it happen; I am deeply indebted. I would also like to thank the team at Pegasus, particularly Claiborne Hancock, Becky Maines, Maria Fernandez, and Heather Rodino.

Most parts of the book were read and reread by Judit Stenn from the very beginning. Not only did she provide generous encouragement, she also provided constructive suggestions regarding the text, structure, and flow; above all she bore unusual restraint over the creative mess both tangible and metaphysical I allegedly generated. For it all, I am grateful.

GLOSSARY

⸺

Alopecia—A general term for any type of hair loss condition; it usually refers to head hair.

Alopecia areata—A specific form of hair loss based on an immune reaction against hair follicles. Alopecia areata occurs in several forms: localized hair loss, head hair loss (alopecia totalis), and total body hair loss (alopecia universalis).

Anagen—The phase of the hair cycle in which the follicle is biggest and the shaft grows.

Androgen—Male hormone.

Androgenetic alopecia—Also called male pattern alopecia or balding. Androgenetic alopecia comes about by the miniaturization of scalp hair follicles; the resultant scalp appears hairless. For this form of alopecia to occur, there must be androgens and a family history of the condition.

Angora—Originally, the name given to a breed of goat with long silky hair. Now the term is applied to any animal with long, silky hair, such as a cat or rabbit.

Appendage (to skin)—A cellular epidermal projection that embellishes skin function, e.g., hair, sweat gland, sebaceous gland, nails.

Archetier or archetierre—The formal name of a violin bow maker, male or female, respectively.

Asynchronous—A term referring to a processes occurring at different times. Asynchronous hair growth describes the situation in which each follicle is cycling independent of its neighboring hair follicle.

Barber-surgeon—An extinct profession that combined the applications of the barber and some of the simple procedures of the surgeon. Important to the barber-surgeon was bloodletting, a procedure debunked and discontinued by the end of the 19th century.

Batt—A layer of carded wool. To form a batt, a portion of wool is placed on a brushing device called a card and a second card is pulled over it. This process is repeated until all the threads are parallel. This organized wool mesh is lifted from the tines of the card as a loose net called a batt.

Beaver—a rodent; also refers to the top hat made of beaver pelt or fur popular in the 17th and 18th centuries.

Bloodletting—One of the activities of the medieval barber, which involved withdrawing blood from an ill person in order to remove imagined disease-causing toxins from the body. A procedure debunked in the 19th century.

Bob—A short hairstyle first popular among women in the early 20th century in which the hair was of even length and extended no lower than the shoulders, but often at the level of the lower ears.

Bristle—The business end of a paintbrush. The hairs were called bristles because originally they came from hogs.

Broadcloth—A fine woolen cloth made on a wide loom.

Carding—The combing of raw wool with a multi-needled brush in order to align the fibers. The original card comb or brush or card was the dried prickly fruit of the thistle (*Carduus*). Cloth finishers used cards to impart a nap on the surface of woven wool cloth. The word "card" is derived from the name of the thistle.

Catagen—The phase of the hair cycle when the follicle stops producing a shaft and undergoes shrinkage of its lower portion.

Clip—The amount of wool sheared from sheep at one time or in one season.

Cortex—The thick central layer of the hair shaft. It consists of tightly bound cells filled with keratin proteins. The cortex provides shaft strength.

Cowlick—A region of the scalp where the hair grows in a spiral pattern; the most common site is the crown, but it may appear anywhere.

Cuticle—Outermost layer of the hair shaft consisting of overlying slatelike cells that point toward the follicle base.

Dermal papilla—A small nubbin of dermis that the lower follicle clasps. The dermal papilla is needed for follicle and hair shaft growth. Alone it can induce follicles from simple epithelium.

Dermis—The layer of skin made of mesenchymal cells that support the epidermis.

Distaff—A stick or staff upon which wool is wound before being made into thread or yarn.

Dreadlock (or "locks")—Long, twisted, felted hair locks made famous by the Rastafarians.

Ectothermy—Cold-bloodedness. Ectothermic animals cannot generate their own body heat so they assume a body temperature of their surroundings.

Endocrine—Describes a gland that puts one or more hormones into the blood.

Endothermy—Warm-bloodedness. Endothermic animals have the ability to generate their own body heat independent of the surroundings.

Epidermis—The outermost portion of skin; it consists of layers of epithelial cells.

Epithelium—Very social cells that tightly bind to one another to form sheets of cells.

External root sheath—The outermost epithelial layer of the hair follicle. This cylindrical layer separates the hair follicle from the surrounding dermis.

Exogen—The phase of the hair follicle cycle during which the hair shaft actively sheds.

Felt—A fabric made by heating, soaping, agitating, and pounding raw wool. Felt fibers are held together by intertwined wool fibers and by the grip of the cuticle.

Ferule—A metal belt on a brush that holds the bristles (the hairs) onto the handle.

Fleece—When shepherds use the term, they are referring to all the wool sheared from one sheep at one time. When clothiers use the term, it refers to a sheepskin or sheep pelt, which consists of wool plus skin.

Follicle—A fingerlike down-growth of epithelial cells from the epidermis that will form the hair shaft factory. Extending off of the follicle is a sebaceous gland and muscle.

Fulling—The act of felting a woven material. The woven material is placed in warm, soapy water and pounded. Afterwards, it is rinsed in water and stretched on a tenter (the person who fulled was also called a walker, waulker, fuller, or tucker).

Genome—All the genetic information of an organism as housed in the sequence of the DNA.

Growth cycle—Biological systems show different growth cycles. The growth cycle for the hair follicle has phases of anagen, catagen, and telogen during which the follicle becomes large then small. The growth cycle for individual cells involves synthesizing cell constituents, such as DNA, and then dividing to form two cells; the cell cycle has phases of growth, rest, and division.

Growth factor—An extracellular small protein that can stimulate a cell to do something such as grow, move, change shape, or produce another growth factor.

Growth factor activator—A growth factor that has a positive effect on a system (for example, it will cause a collection of cells to form a kidney).

Growth factor inhibitor—A growth factor that has a negative effect on a system (for example, it will prevent a collection of cells from forming a kidney).

Growth pattern—The unique set of positions hairs take on a person's head and body.

Guild—In medieval times, a union of specialized craftsmen that served to set standards and protection for the trade.

Hair—In the world of hair, the word may refer to hair shafts alone or hair follicles and shafts. In this book, the word "hair" refers only to the shaft, but we are also using "hair" to refer to fur, wool, whiskers, and quills.

Hank—A bundle of loose hair.

Heddle—Wires or hooks serving to separate the warp threads of a loom in order to make a shed through which weft threads (on a shuttle) will pass. Heddles facilitated the weaving of complex cloth patterns.

Internal (inner) root sheath—The layer of the hair follicle that holds the hair shaft on its way out. The internal root sheath is itself surrounded by the outer, or external, root sheath.

Keratin—A large family of thread-shaped proteins that fill keratinocyte cytoplasm. Keratin-filled cells make up the hair follicle and shaft and bestow on the cell tensile strength.

Macaroni—This term refers to the dandies who returned to England after a European tour, which included learning about pasta and an outlandish way of dress (including wigs).

Made-beaver—Beaver pelt (skin plus fur) that had been worn for a period of time resulting in pelt softening and removal of overfur hairs.

Male pattern baldness—An androgen-dependent familial condition associated with minimization of hair follicles over the head in defined patterns. The areas of follicle minimization appear "bald."

Marcel waves—Hair waves formed by a heated curling iron and clamp invented by Marcel Grateau.

Melanocyte—A cell that manufactures melanin pigment and packages it into melanosomes. The melanocyte transfers pigment by long branching cell process to hair shaft keratinocytes.

Melanogenesis—The process of melanin pigment production.

Melanosomes—Small packets of melanin pigment kept in the cytoplasm of melanocytes until it is passed on to keratinocytes.

***Memento mori* pieces**—Latin term meaning "remember you must die" applied to jewelry that commemorates a deceased person.

Mercer—A dealer in textiles.

Merchant-banker—The term is used in this book to refer to the agents who financed the trade of wool.

Merino sheep—A sheep breed that arose in Spain but now makes up flocks worldwide.

Merkin—Pubic hair wig.

Mesenchymal (mesenchyme) cell—A cell present in animal connective tissue such as the dermis. These cells make proteinaceous matrix materials such as collagen, cartilage, and bone.

Mesenchyme—Connective tissue that makes up the dermis.

Muscle of the hair follicle—A thin muscle attached to the mid-portion of the anagen follicle, which, when stimulated, pulls the follicle upright and the hair shaft erect.

Nap—The hairy surface of a cloth formed by short hairs usually pulled up out of the weave by a brushing process often using a teasel; the pile of a cloth.

Outer (external) root sheath—The outermost layer of the hair follicle, which separates the follicle from the surrounding dermis.

Overcoat fur (overfur)—The long, relatively sparsely placed hair shafts that lie over the densely packed underfur of a furred animal.

Patterning (biological)—The arrangement of cells and tissues with respect to one another and the larger environment.

Pelt—Animal skin with fur or wool still attached.

Periwig—British term for a wig used in the 17th and 18th century. It referred specifically to a men's wig pulled back into a queue.

Peruke—French term from which "periwig" is derived.

Pheomelanin—The cell pigment produced by melanocytes that gives red color to hair.

Pigmentation—Coloration of hair follicle cells due to melanin or pheomelanin pigments.

Pomade—A scented ointment used to facilitate the grooming of hair. Pomade makes the hair look shiny, slick, and neat. In the past, pomades contained beeswax, petroleum jelly, and lard.

Queue—A braid of hair hanging from the back of the head, a pigtail.

Quill—Long, sharp, spiny hairs of the porcupine or hedgehog.

Raw wool—Wool in its natural condition, taken directly from a sheep without any processing.

Regenerative medicine—The medical specialty studying how to regenerate injured, diseased, or absent organs and tissues.

Scourer—The person who washes raw wool.

Sebaceous gland—A gland that empties oil into the follicle canal, thereby lubricating the hair shaft, which in turn carries oil to the skin surface.

Sebum—The oily material produced by sebaceous glands.

Sensory organ—A structure that is well endowed with nerves that serve to detect a change in the surroundings.

Shaft—The filament produced by a hair follicle made of epithelial cells filled with keratin protein. Hair shaft cells are fossilized and thus unable to grow or sense the surroundings.

Shearer—The person who cuts wool from sheep.

Shed—Space opened up in the warp threads by the heddle to allow the shuttle to pass through.

Shuttle—The small device holding weft thread. In a full loom the weaver passes the shuttle under the uplifted warp fibers.

Spindle—A tapered wooden rod, weighted at its bottom and used to twist fibers into thread.

Spinsters—The name given to the people who spun thread, often the women of the house.

Stem cell—A cell having the ability to divide and form two cells. One cell reproduces the stem cell and the second re-forms the tissue or organ in which the stem cells rests. Stems cells have varying ability to regenerate tissue: Some can reform a whole embryo and others can regenerate only one tissue, such as bone.

Sulfur bonds—A chemical link between two chemical atoms each extending off a separate protein. Sulfur bonds form between cysteine groups on adjacent proteins.

Synchronous—A term referring to processes occurring at the same time. Synchronous hair growth describes the situation in which all the hair follicles are in the same phase of the cycle at any point of time.

Teasel—The prickly fruit of the teasel plant, which was used to comb (card) wool.

Telogen—The resting phase of the hair cycle.

Tenter—A frame on which cloth is stretched to dry evenly.

Tenterhook—Hooked nails on the tenter that hold the cloth during the drying process.

Terminal hair follicle—A large hair follicle such as one from the head, which produces a thick, long, and colored shaft.

Tinea capitis—An infection of the scalp by a form of hair-eating fungus.

Thread—Long-fibered wool tightly spun.

Thyroid hormone—An endocrine hormone liberated by the thyroid gland (this gland sits on the breathing tube at the level of the voice box).

Tissue (biological)—A collection of unique cells making up the substance of an organ, such as fat tissue, bone tissue, cartilage tissue, liver tissue.

Tissue (cell) culture—The technique of growing cells from any animal tissue in a laboratory flask.

Tonsorial—Of or related to barbering.

Tonsure—Clipping or shaving off portions of scalp hair in celebration of a clerical or monastic state.

Transplant—The surgical process of moving tissue from one site to another.

For a hair transplant, the surgeon moves hair follicles from the side of the scalp to the bald spot.

Tress—A lock of human hair.

Undercoat fur (underfur)—The very thin, short, curled, or straight hair in high density over the skin of most non-primate mammals. It is overlaid by long, thick hair fibers: the overhairs.

Vellus hair follicle—A short hair follicle that makes a thin, short hair fiber no thicker than two to three red blood cells. These hairs cover areas of the body that appear "hairless," such as the forehead or nose.

Warp—The vertical threads of a loom. In the simplest weave the weft thread is passed alternately over and under the warp threads. This process is assisted by heddles, which raise the warp threads to give a space, a shed, for the weft thread.

Warp-weighted loom (primitive, vertical)—The original looms were vertical, where the warp threads ran down. These threads were kept down by tying weights to their ends.

Weaving—The process of binding horizontal weft threads into an array of vertical warp threads.

Weaving loom—A frame for holding warp threads parallel to permit the interlacing of the right-angled weft threads to form a web. A true loom also contains a heddle, which lifts warp fibers to make the shed.

Weft (weaving)—The yarns or thread carried horizontally back and forth in the weaving process.

Weft (wigs)—A strip of hair woven onto strings that will then be incorporated into a wig. The term weft also refers to the strip of hair placed on the eyelid (an eyelid wig).

Whisker—Refers to hairs on the face, upper lip, chin, cheeks. It also refers to the vibrissae, primarily sensory structures, which are located on the upper lip of most mammals.

Wig block—a head-shaped block made of wood or canvas stuffed with sawdust and used to mount wigs for styling or construction.

Wig foundation (or base, or net)—A head-shaped net or lace into which hairs are tied to make a wig.

Wool—Fur clipped from sheep.

Woolens—Woven or knitted materials made of yarn. These materials usually have a nap.

Worsted Thread—A very tightly spun wool thread made of long fibers.

Worsteds—Cloth woven from worsted thread. This cloth has no nap and the woven pattern is easily seen in the finished cloth (unlike the hidden woven pattern in a fulled cloth).

Yarn—Loosely spun threads made of short wool fibers.

SELECTED BIBLIOGRAPHY

—

Agrawal P and Barat GK. "Utilization of Human Hair in Animal Feed." *Agricultural Wastes* 17, 1986: 53–58.

Ahmad W, Faiyaz ul Haque M, Brancolini V, Tsou HC, ul Haque S, Lam H, Aita VM, Owen J, deBlaquiere M, Frank J, Cserhalmi-Friedman PB, Leask A, McGrath JA, Peacocke M, Ahmad M, Ott J, Christiano AM. "Alopecia Universalis Associated with a Mutation in the Human Hairless Gene." *Science* 279, 1998: 720–724.

Albers KM and Davis BM. "The Skin as a Neurotropic Organ." *The Neuroscientist* 13, 2007: 371–382.

Alibardi L. "Perspectives on Hair Evolution Based on Some Comparative Studies on Vertebrate Cornification." *Journal of Experimental Zoology* 381B, 2012: 325–343.

Amoh Y, Li L, Katsuoka K, and Hoffman RM. "Multipotent Hair Follicle Stem Cells Promote Repair of Spinal Cord Injury and Recovery of Walking Function." *Cell Cycle* 7, 2008: 1865–1869.

Auber L. "The Anatomy of the Follicles Producing Wool-Fibers, with Special Reference to Keratinization." *Transactions of the Royal Society* 62 (Part 1), 1950–1951: 191–254.

Beaton AA and Mellor G. "Direction of Hair Whorl And Handedness." *Laterality* 12, 2007: 295–301.

Beck M. "Medical Spas Get a Checkup. States Weigh Tighter Rules on Cosmetic-Procedure Centers After Patient Injuries." *Wall Street Journal*, June 5, 2013, A3.

Bell A. *Hair*. Newark, New Jersey: Paul Robson Galleries, Rutgers University Press, 2013.

Bell AR, Brooks C, and Dryburgh PR. *The English Wool Market 1230–1327*. Cambridge: Cambridge University Press, 2007.

Bell CJ. *Collector's Encyclopedia of Hairwork Jewelry*. Paducah, KY: Collector Books, 1998.

Benjamin J. *Starting to Collect Antique Jewellery*. Suffolk, England: Antique Collectors' Club, 2003.

Bianco J, Cateforis D, Heartney E, Hockley A, and Kennedy B. *Wenda Gu at Dartmouth: The Art of Installation*. Hanover, NH: University Press of New England, 2008.

Biddle-Perry G and Cheang, S, editors. *Hair: Styling, Culture and Fashion*. Oxford, England: Berg Publishers, 2008.

Bilefsky D. "In Albanian Feuds, Isolation Engulfs Families." *New York Times*, July 10, 2008.

Binkley C. "Which Outfit Is Greenest? A New Rating Tool." *Wall Street Journal*, July 12, 2012.

Bloch RH. *A Needle in the Right Hand of God. The Norman Conquest of 1066 and the Making and Meaning of the Bayeux Tapestry*. New York: Random House, 2006.

Botchkarev, VA. "Stress and the Hair Follicle: Exploring the Connections." *American Journal of Pathology* 162, 2003: 709–712.

Botham M and Sharrad L. *Manual of Wigmaking*. London: Heinemann, 1964.

Bradford E. *English Victorian Jewelry*. Norwich, England: Spring Books, 1959.

Broudy E. *The Book of Looms*. Hanover, NH: Brown University Press, 1979.

Brown S, Dent A, Martens C, and McQuaid M. *Fashioning Felt*. New York: Smithsonian Institution, 2009.

Brownell I, Guevara E, Bai CB, Loomis CA, and Joyner AL. "Nerve-Derived Sonic Hedgehog Defines a Niche for Hair Follicle Stem Cells Capable of Becoming Epidermal Stem Cells." *Cell Stem Cell* 8, 2011: 552–565.

Bryer R. *The History of Hair: Fashion and Fantasy Down the Ages*. London: Philip Wilson Publishers, 2000.

Bunn S. *Nomadic Felts*. London: The British Museum Press, 2010.

Campbell M. *Self-Instructor in the Art of Hair Work, Dressing Hair, Making Curls, Switches, Braids, and Hair Jewelry of Every Description*. New York: M. Campbell, 1867.

Chapman DM. "The Anchoring Strengths of Various Chest Hair Root Types." *Clinical Experimental Dermatology* 17, 1992: 421–423.

Cheang S. "Roots: Hair and Race" in *Hair: Styling, Culture and Fashion*. Editors G Biddle-Perry and S Cheang,. Oxford, MS: Berg Publications, 2007.

Chen KG, Mallon BS, McKay RDG, and Robey PG. "Human Pluripotent Stem Cell Culture: Consideration for Maintenance, Expansion and Therapeutics." *Cell Stem Cell* 14, 2014: 13–26.

Cherel Y, Kernaleguen L, Richard P, and Guinet G. "Whisker Isotopic Signature Depicts Migration Patterns and Multi-year Intra- and Inter-individual Foraging Strategies in Fur Seals." *Biology Letters* 5, 2009: 830–832.

Chernow R. *Titan: The Life of John D. Rockefeller, Sr.* New York: Random House, 1998.

Churchill, JE. *The Complete Book of Tanning Skins and Furs*. Mechanicsburg, PA: Stackpole Books, 1983. E-book.

Constantine M and Larsen JL. *Beyond Craft: The Art Fabric*. New York: Van Nostrand Reinhold Company, 1972.

Cossins AR and Bowler K. *Temperature Biology of Animals*. London: Chapman and Hall, 1987: Chapter 1.

Cremer L. *The Physics of the Violin*. Cambridge, MA: The MIT Press, 1984: 1–4.

Critchley M. *The Dyslexic Child*. London: Heinemann, 1970: 69.

Darwin, C. 1845. *Voyage of the Beagle*. New York: Modern Library, 2001.

Darwin, C. 1871. *Descent of Man*. New York: Penguin Random House, 2004.

D'Aulaire I and D'Aulaire EP. *Book of Greek Myths*. New York: Bantam Doubleday Dell, 1962.

Daves J. *Medieval Sheep and the Wool Trade: Sheep, Wool and the Wool Trade in the Middle Ages*. Bristol: Stuart Press, 2008.

Davies NB, Krebs JRE, and West SA. *An Introduction to Behavioral Ecology, Fourth Edition*. Hoboken, NJ: Wiley-Blackwell, 2012.

Dawber R. *Diseases of the Scalp*. Third Edition. Oxford: Blackwell Science Publishers, 1982.

Dean I and Siva-Jothy MT. "Human Fine Body Hair Enhances Ectoparasite Detection." *Biology Letters* 8, 2012: 358–361.

Deetz J. *In Small Things Forgotten*. New York: Doubleday, 1996.

Dhouailly D. "A New Scenario for the Evolutionary Origin of Hair, Feather, and Avian Scales." *Journal of Anatomy* 214, 2009: 587–606.

Dikotter F. "Hairy Barbarians, Furry Primates and Wild Men: Medical Science and Cultural Representations of Hair in China" in *Hair: Its Power and Meaning in Asian Cultures.* Editors A Hiltebeitel and BD Miller. New York Press: Albany State University, 1998.

Dolan EJ. *Fur, Fortune and Empire: The Epic History of the Fur Trade in America.* New York: W. W. Norton and Company, 2010.

Domingo-Roura X, Marmi J, Ferrando A, et al. "Badger Hair in Shaving Brushes Comes from Protected Eurasian Badgers." *Biological Conservation* 128, 2006: 425–430.

Donkin RA. "Cistercian Sheep-Farming and Wool Sales in the Thirteenth Century." *Agricultural History Review* 6, 1958: 2–8.

Dutton D. *The Art Instinct. Beauty, Pleasure and Human Evolution.* New York: Bloomsbury Press, 2009.

Eccles WJ. *The Canadian Frontier 1534–1760.* Albuquerque, NM: University of New Mexico Press, 1983.

Eckhart L, Valle LD, Jaeger K, et al. "Identification of Reptilian Genes Encoding Hair Keratin-Like Proteins Suggests a New Scenario for the Evolutionary Origin of Hair." *Proceedings of the National Academy of Sciences* 105, 2008: 18419–18423.

Elias H and Bortner S. "On the Phylogeny of Hair." *American Museum Novitates* 1820, 1957:1–15.

Feughelman M and Willis BK. "Mechanical Extension of Human Hair and the Movement of the Cuticle." *Journal of Cosmetic Science* 52, 2001: 185–193.

Fischer DH. *Champlain' s Dream.* New York: Simon & Schuster, 2008.

Fletcher AJ. *Ancient Egyptian Hair.* Manchester: University of Manchester Press, 1995.

Francis K and Morantz T. *Partners in Furs: A History of the Fur Trade in Eastern James Bay 1600–1870.* Montreal: McGill-Queen's University Press, 1983.

Fraser RDB and MacRae TP. "Molecular Structure and Mechanical Properties of Keratins" in *The Mechanical Properties of Biological Materials.* Editors JF Vincent and JD Currey. Cambridge: Cambridge University Press, 1980: 211–246.

Frazer JG. *The Golden Bough: A Study in Magic and Religion.* New York: Macmillan, 1952.

Frosch D. "A Lonely and Bleak Existence in the West, Tending the Flock." *New York Times*, February 22, 2009.

Galbraith K. "Back in Style: The Fur Trade." *New York Times*, December 24, 2006.

Garza LA, Yang CC, Zhao T, Blatt HB, et al. "Bald Scalp in Men with Androgenetic Alopecia Retains Hair Follicle Stem Cells but Lacks CD200-Rich and CD34-Positive Hair Follicle Progenitor Cells." *Journal of Clinical Investigation* 121, 2011: 613–622.

Garza LA, Liu Y, Yang Z, Alagesan B, et al. "Prostaglandin D2 Inhibits Hair Growth and Is Elevated in Bald Scalp of Men with Androgenetic Alopecia." *Science Translational Medicine* 4, 2012: 126–134.

Gilchrist J. *The Church and Economic Activity in the Middle Ages*. London: St. Martin's Press, 1969.

Gill FB. *Ornithology, Second Edition*. New York: W.H. Freeman and Company, 1995.

Gilmeister H. *Tennis: A Cultural History*. London: Leicester University Press, 1997.

Gjecov S. *The Code of Leke Dukagjini (The Kanun)*. New York: Gjonkelaj Publishing Company, 1989.

Gordon B. *Feltmaking*. New York: Watson-Guptill Publications, 1980.

Gurdon JB and Bourillot P-Y. "Morphogen Gradient Interpretation." *Nature* 413, 2001: 797–803.

Hanson T. *Feathers: The Evolution of a Natural Miracle*. New York: Basic Books, 2011.

Hardy MH. "The Secret Life of the Hair Follicle." *Trends in Genetics* 8, 1992: 55–61.

Harran S and Harran J. "Hair Jewelry." *Antique Week*, December 1997.

Harris B. "The Mechanical Behavior of Composite Materials" in *The Mechanical Properties of Biological Materials*. Editors JF Vincent and JD Currey. Cambridge: Cambridge University Press, 1980: 37–74.

Hausman LA. "A Comparative Racial Study of the Structural Elements of Human Head-Hair." *American Naturalist* 59, 1925: 529–538.

Haywood J. *Historical Atlas of the Vikings*. London: Penguin Books, 1995.

Hearle JWS. "A Critical Review of the Structural Mechanics of Wool and Hair Fibres." *International Journal of Biological Macromolecules* 27, 2000: 123–138.

Heidenreich DE and Ray AJ. *The Early Fur Trades: A Study in Cultural Interaction*. Toronto: McClelland and Stewart, 1976.

Henderson FV. *How to Make a Violin Bow.* Seattle: Murray Publishing Company, 1977.

Higuchi R, von Beroldingen CH, Sensabaugh GF, and Erhlich HA. "DNA Typing from Single Hairs." *Nature* 332, 1988: 543–546.

Hiltebeitel A and Miller BD, editors. *Hair: Its Power and Meaning in Asian Cultures.* Albany: State University of New York Press, 1998.

International Society of Hair Restoration Surgeons (ISHRS) 2013. *International Society of Hair Restoration Surgery: 2013 Practice Census Results.* www.ishrs.org.

International Wool Textile Organization. http://www.iwto.org/wool/history-of-wool.

Ito M, Yang Z, Andl T, Cui C, et al. "Wnt-Dependent De Novo Hair Follicle Regeneration in Adult Mouse Skin after Wounding." *Nature* 447, 2007: 316–320.

Jablonski NG. *Skin: A Natural History.* Berkeley: University of California Press, 2006.

Jablonski NG. "The Naked Truth: Why Humans Have No Fur." *Scientific American* 302, 2010: 42–49.

Jenkins JG, editor. *The Textile Industry in Great Britain.* London: Routledge & Kegan Paul Publishers, 1972.

Jessen KR, Mirsky R, and Arthur-Farraj P. "The Role of Cell Plasticity in Tissue Repair: Adaptive Cellular Reprogramming." *Developmental Cell* 34, 2015: 613-620.

Jolly PH. *Hair: Untangling a Social History.* East Long Meadow, MA: The John Ce Otto Printing Company, 2004.

Jordan M. "Hair Matters in South Central Africa" in *Hair in African Art and Culture.* Editors R Sieber and F Herreman. Munich: Prestel Verlag, 2000: 135.

Kalabokes VD. "Alopecia Areata: Support Groups and Meetings—How Can It Help Your Patient?" *Dermatologic Therapy* 24, 2011: 302–304.

Kamberov YG, Wang S, Tan J, et al. "Modeling Recent Human Evolution in Mice by Expression of a Selected EDAR Variant." *Cell* 152, 2013: 691–702.

Kazantseva A, Goltsov A, Zinchenko R, et al. "Human Hair Growth Deficiency Is Linked to a Genetic Defect in the Phospholipase Gene LIPH." *Science* 314, 2006: 982–985.

Khumalo NP, Dawber RPR, and Ferguson DJP. "Apparent Fragility of African Hair Is Unrelated to the Cystine-Rich Protein Distribution: A Cytochemical Electron Microscope Study." *Experimental Dermatology* 14, 2005: 311–314.

Kingdon J, Agwanda B, Kinnaird M, O'Brien T, et al. "A Poisonous Surprise

Under the Coat of the African Crested Rat." *Proceedings of the Royal Society* B 279, 2012: 675–680.

Kittler R, Kayser M, and Stoneking M. "Molecular Evolution of Pediculus Humanus and the Origin of Clothing." *Current Biology* 13, 2003: 1414–1417.

Kramer AE and Revkin AC. "Arctic Shortcut, Long a Dream, Beckons Shippers as Ice Thaws." *New York Times*, September 11, 2009.

Kübler-Ross E and Kessler D. *On Grief and Grieving: Finding the Meaning of Grief Through the Five Stages of Loss.* New York: Scribner, 2005.

Langbein L and Schweizer J. "Keratins of the Human Hair Follicle." *International Review of Cytology* 243, 2005: 1–78.

Laut AC. *The Fur Trade of America.* New York: Macmillan, 1921.

Leavitt D. *The Man Who Knew Too Much: Alan Turing and the Invention of the Computer.* New York: W. W. Norton & Company, 2006.

Lee YR, Lee SJ, Kim JC, and Ogawa H. "Hair Restoration Surgery in Patients with Pubic Atrichosis or Hypotrichosis: Review of Technique and Clinical Consideration of 507 Cases." *Dermatologic Surgery* 32, 2006: 1327–1335.

Le Fur Y. *Cheveux cheris. Frivolites et trophees.* Paris: Musee du Quai Branly, 2013.

Leggett WF. *The Story of Wool.* Brooklyn: Chemical Publishing Company, 1947.

Lennon C. "Preshampoo Is Not a Sham." *Wall Street Journal*, February 6, 2013.

Li L, Rutlin M, Abraira VE, Cassidy C, et al. "The Functional Organization of Cutaneous Low-Threshold Mechanosensory Neurons." *Cell* 247, 2011: 1615–1627.

Li L and Clevers H. "Coexistence of Quiescent and Active Adult Stem Cells in Mammals." *Science* 327, 2010: 542–545.

Li W, Li K, Wei W, and Ding S. "Chemical Approaches to Stem Cell Biology and Therapeutics." *Cell Stem Cell* 13, 2013: 270–283.

Lipson E. *A Short History of Wool and Its Manufacture.* Cambridge, MA: Harvard University Press, 1953.

Livesey R and AG Smith. *The Fur Traders.* Markham: Fitzhenry & Whiteside, 1989: 77.

Lloyd TH. *The English Wool Trade in the Middle Ages.* Cambridge, MA: Harvard University Press, 1977.

Loussouarn G. "African Hair Growth Parameters." *British Journal of Dermatology* 145, 2001: 294–297.

Loussouarn G, Garcel A-L, Lozano I, Collaudin C, et al. "Worldwide Diversity of Hair Curliness: A New Method of Assessment." *International Journal of Dermatology* 46, 2007: Suppl 1: 2–6.

Maderson PFA. "When? Why? And How? Some Speculations on the Evolution of the Vertebrate Integument." *American Zoologist* 12, 1972: 159–171.

Mann GB, Fowler KJ, Gabriel A, et al. "Mice with a Null Mutation of the TGF-Alpha Gene Have Abnormal Skin Architecture, Wavy Hair and Curly Whiskers and Often Develop Corneal Inflammation." *Cell* 73, 1993: 249–261.

Maurer M, Peters EMJ, Botchkarev VA, and Paus R. "Intact Hair Follicle Innervation Is Not Essential for Anagen Induction and Development." *Archives of Dermatological Research* 290, 1998: 574–578.

Menkart J, Wolfram LJ, and Mao I. "Caucasian Hair, Negro Hair and Wool: Similarities and Differences." *Journal of the Society of Cosmetic Chemists* 17, 1966: 769–787.

Miller J. "Hair Without a Head: Disembodiment and the Uncanny" in *Hair Styling, Culture and Fashion*. Editors G Biddle-Perry and S Cheang. Oxford: Berg Publications, 2008.

Mollett AL. *York's Golden Fleece: History of Wool Trade*. Whitby: Horne and Son, 1962.

Montagna W, Prota G, and Kenney JA Jr. *Black Skin: Structure and Function*. San Diego: Academic Press, 1993.

Morison, SE. *The European Discovery of America: The Northern Voyages*. New York: Oxford University Press, 1971.

Morris D. *Naked Ape: A Zoologist's Study of the Human Animal*. New York: Random House, 1967.

Morse EW. *Fur Trade Canoe Routes of Canada: Then and Now*. Toronto: University of Toronto Press, 1971.

Mou C, Jackson B, Schneider P, Overbeek PA, and Headon DJ. "Generation of the Primary Hair Follicle Pattern." *Proceedings of the National Academy of Sciences* 103, 2006: 9075–9080.

Munro JH. *Textiles, Towns and Trade: Essays in the Economic History of Late-Medieval England and the Low Countries*. Ashgate: Variorum Publishing Ltd., 1994.

Murray EA. *Trails of Evidence: How Forensic Science Works*. Chantilly: The Teaching Company, 2012.

Nagorcka BN and Mooney JR. "The Role of a Reaction-Diffusion System in the Formation of Hair Fibres." *Journal of Theoretical Biology* 98, 1982: 575–607.

Nagorcka BN and Mooney JR. "The Role of a Reaction-Diffusion System in the Initiation of Primary Hair Follicles." *Journal of Theoretical Biology* 114, 1985: 243–272.

Nagorcka BN and Mooney JR. "Spatial Patterns Produced by a Reaction-Diffusion System in Primary Hair Follicles." *Journal of Theoretical Biology* 115, 1985: 299–317.

Nakamura M, Schneider MR, Schmidt-Ullrich R, Paus, R. "Mutant Laboratory Mice with Abnormalities in Hair Follicle Morphogenesis, Cycling, and/or Structure: An Update." *Journal of Dermatologic Science* 69, 2012: 6–29.

Nishimura EK, Granter SR, and Fisher DE. "Mechanisms of Hair Graying: Incomplete Melanocyte Stem Cell Maintenance in the Niche." *Science* 307, 2005: 720–724.

O'Callaghan JF. *A History of Medieval Spain*. Cornell: Cornell University Press, 1976.

Ockenga S. *On Women and Friendship: A Collection of Victorian Keepsakes and Traditions*. New York: Stuart, Tabori & Chang Publishing, 1993.

Oliver RF. "Whisker Growth After Removal of the Dermal Papilla and Lengths of Follicle in the Hooded Rat." *Journal of Embryology and Experimental Morphology* 15, 1966: 331–347.

Orientreich N. "Autografts in Alopecias and Other Selected Dermatological Conditions." *Annals of the New York Academy of Sciences* 83, 1959: 463.

Oshima H, Rochat A, Kedzia C, Kobayashi K, and Barrandon Y. "Morphogenesis and Renewal of Hair Follicles from Adult Multipotent Stem Cells." *Cell* 104, 2001: 233–245.

Pannekoek F. *The Fur Trade and Western Canadian Society, 1670–1870*. Ottawa: Canadian Historical Association, 1987.

Papakostas D, Rancan F, Sterry W. et al. "Nanoparticles in Dermatology." *Archives of Dermatologic Research* 303, 2013: 533–550.

Parliament UK. "Woolsack." http://www.parliament.uk/site-information/glossary/woolsack.

Peters EMJ, Arck PC, and Paus R. "Hair Growth Inhibition by Psychoemotional Stress: A Mouse Model for Neural Mechanisms in Hair Growth Control." *Experimental Dermatology* 15, 2006: 1–13.

Petukova L, Duvic M, Hordinsky M, Norris D, Price V, et al. "Genome-Wide Association Study in Alopecia Areata Implicates Both Innate and Adaptive Immunity." *Nature* 466, 2010: 113–117.

Phillips CR and Phillips WD Jr. *Spain's Golden Fleece: Wool Production and the Wool Trade from the Middle Ages to the Nineteenth Century*. Baltimore: The Johns Hopkins University Press, 1997.

Phillips PC. *The Fur Trade: Volume 1.* Norman: University of Oklahoma Press, 1961.

Pleij H. *Colors Demonic and Divine: Shade of Meaning in the Middle Ages and After.* New York: Columbia University Press, 2004.

Plikus M, Mayer JA, de la Cruz D, Baker RE, et al. "Cyclic Dermal BMP Signaling Regulates Stem Cell Activation During Hair Regeneration." *Nature* 451, 2008: 340–344.

Plikus MV, Gay DL, Treffeisen E, Wang A, et al. "Epithelial Stem Cells and Implications for Wound Repair." *Seminars in Cell Developmental Biology* 23, 2012: 946–953.

Plummer W. "Her Kind of Beauty." *People*, August 11, 1997.

Popescu C and Hocker H. "Hair—The Most Sophisticated Biological Composite Material." *Chemical Society Reviews* 36, 2007: 1282–1291.

Porter C, Diridollou S, and Barbosa VH. "The Influence of African-American Hair's Curl Pattern on Its Mechanical Properties." *International Journal of Dermatology* 44, 2005: Suppl 1: 4–5.

Power E. *The Wool Trade in English Medieval History.* Oxford: Oxford University Press, 1941.

Rauser A. "Hair, Authenticity, and the Self-Made Macaroni." *Eighteenth Century Studies* 38, 2004: 101–117.

Reddy K and Lowenstein EJ. "Forensics in Dermatology: Part II." *Journal of the American Academy of Dermatology* 64, 2011: 811–824.

Redgrove HS. *Hair-Dyes and Hair-Dyeing Chemistry and Technique.* London: William Heinemann, 1939.

Rieu EV, translator. *Homer: The Odyssey.* New York: Penguin Books, 1948.

Rinn JL, Bondre C, Gladstone HB, Brown PO, and Chang H. "Anatomic Demarcation by Positional Variation in Fibroblast Gene Expression Programs." *PLoS (Public Library of Science) Genetics* 2, 2006: 1084–1096.

Robbins, CR. *Chemical and Physical Behavior of Human Hair, Fourth Edition.* New York: Springer-Verlag, 2002.

Robertson JR. *Forensic Examination of Hair.* Boca Raton, FL: CRC Publishing, 1999.

Rocaboy F. "The Structure of Bow-Hair Fibers." *Catgut Acoustic Society Journal* 1, 1990: 34–36.

Roersma ME, Douven LFA, Lefki K, and Oomens CWJ. "The Failure Behavior of the Anchorage of Hairs During Slow Extraction." *Journal of Biomechanics* 34, 2001: 319–325.

Roesdahl E. *The Vikings*. London: The Penguin Press, 1987.

Rogers AR, Iltis D, and Wooding S. "Genetic Variation at the MC1R Locus and the Time Since Loss of Human Body Hair." *Current Anthropology* 45, 2004: 105–108.

Rogers GE. "Biology of the Wool Follicle: An Excursion into a Unique Tissue Interaction System Waiting to be Rediscovered." *Experimental Dermatology* 15, 2006: 931–949.

Rogers MA, Langbein L, Praetzel-Wunder S, Winter H, and Schweizer J. "Human Hair Keratin-Associated Proteins (KAPS)." *International Review of Cytology* 251, 2006: 209–263.

Rompolas P, Deschene ER, Zito G, Gonzalez DG, et al. "Live Imaging of Stem Cells and Progeny Behaviour in Physiological Hair-Follicle Regeneration." *Nature* 487, 2012: 496–499.

Rosenbaum M and Leibel RL. "Adaptive Thermogenesis in Humans." *International Journal of Obesity* 34, 2010: 547–555.

Ross CD. *The Influence of the West Country Wool Trade on the Social and Economic History of England*. London: Department of Education of the International Wool Secretariat, 1955.

Rossin L. Linda Rossin Studios, Oak Ridge, NJ. Personal interview. July 29, 2013.

Rousseau I. "Who, Or What, Killed Napoleon?" http://www.cbsnews.com/stories/2002/10/30/tech/main527531.shtml.

Ruskai M and Lowery A. *Wig Making and Styling*. Amsterdam: Elsevier Publishing, 2010.

Ryder ML. "Medieval Sheep and Wool Types." *Agricultural History Review* 32, 1984: 14–28.

Sandoz M. *The Beaver Men: Spearheads of Empire*. New York: Hastings House Publishing, 1964.

Sato I, Nakaki S, Murata K, Takeshita H, and Mukai T. "Forensic Hair Analysis to Identify Animal Species in a Case of Pet Animal Abuse." *International Journal of Legal Medicine* 124, 2010: 249–256.

Scali-Sheahan M, editor. *Milady's STANDARD Professional Barbering*. Fifth Edition. Clifton Park, NY: Cengage Learning Publishing, 2011.

Schoeser M. *World Textiles: A Concise History*. London: Thames & Hudson Ltd, 2003.

Schwalm M. Barber Styling Institute, Camp Hill, Pennsylvania. Personal interview. June 6, 2013.

Schweizer J, Langbein L, Rogers MA, and Winter H. "Hair Follicle Specific Keratins and Their Diseases." *Experimental Cell Research* 313, 2007: 2010–2020.

Sennett R and Rendl M. "Mesenchymal-Epithelial Interactions During Hair Follicle Morphogenesis and Cycling." *Seminars in Cell and Developmental Biology* 23, 2012: 917–927.

Severn B. *The Long and Short of It: Five Thousand Years of Fun and Fury over Hair.* New York: David McKay Company, 1971.

Shaak E. Mount Airy Violins and Bows. Philadelphia. Personal interview. June 12, 2013.

Shakespeare W. "That time of year thou mayst in me behold," Sonnet 73 in *The Art of Shakespeare's Sonnets.* Cambridge, MA: Harvard University Press, 1997.

Sharpe PT. "Fish Scale Development: Hair Today, Teeth and Scales Yesterday?" *Current Biology* 11, 2001: R751–R752.

Sherrow V. *Encyclopedia of Hair: A Cultural History.* Westport: Greenwood Press, 2006.

Sheumaker H. *Love Entwined: The Curious History of Hair Work in America.* Philadelphia: University of Pennsylvania Press, 2007.

Sholley M and Cotran R. "Endothelial DNA Synthesis in the Microvasculature of Rat Skin During the Hair Growth Cycle." *American Journal of Anatomy* 147, 1976: 243–254.

Sick S, Reinker S, Timmer J, and Schlake T. "WNT and DKK Determine Hair Follicle Spacing Through a Reaction Diffusion Mechanism." *Science* 314, 2006: 1447–1450.

Sieber R and Herreman F. *Hair in African Art and Culture.* New York: Museum for African Art, 2000.

Silva JE. "Physiological Importance and Control of Non-Shivering Facultative Thermogenesis." *Frontiers in Bioscience* 3, 2011: 352–371.

Spufford P. *Power and Profit: The Merchant in Medieval Europe.* London: Thames and Hudson Inc., 2002.

Stellar R. *Fur Farming Industry and Trade Summary. 1998–2002.* http://www.usitc.gov/publications/332/pub3666.pdf.

Stenn KS & Paus R. "Controls of Hair Follicle Cycling." *Physiological Reviews* 81, 2001: 449–494.

Stenn KS, Zheng Y, Parimoo S. "Phylogeny of the Hair Follicle: The Sebogenic Hypothesis." *Journal of Investigative Dermatology* 138, 2008: 1576–1578.

Stoddard DM. *The Scented Ape: The Biology and Culture of Human Odour.* Cambridge: Cambridge University Press, 1990.

Sundberg,JP. *Handbook of Mouse Mutations with Skin and Hair Abnormalities: Abnormal Models and Biomedical Tools.* Boca Raton, FL: CRC Press, 1994.

Sutou S. "Hairless Mutation: A Driving Force of Humanization from a Human-Ape Common Ancestor Enforcing Upright Walking While Holding a Baby with Both Hands." *Genes Cells* 17, 2012: 263–272.

Terrien J, Perret M, and Aujard F. "Behavioral Thermoregulation in Mammals: A Review." *Frontiers in Bioscience* 16, 2001: 1428–1444.

Thibaut S, Barbarat P, Leroy F, and Bernard BA. "Human Hair Keratin Network and Curvature." *International Journal of Dermatology* 46, 2007: Suppl 1: 7–10.

Thibaut S, De Becker E, Caisey L. Baras D, et al. "Human Eyelash Characterization." *British Journal of Dermatology* 162, 2009: 304–310.

Tobin DJ. "Human Hair Pigmentation—Biological Aspects." *International Journal of Cosmetic Science* 30, 2008: 233–257.

Tobin DJ. "The Cell Biology of Human Hair Follicle Pigmentation." *Pigment Cell Melanoma Research* 24, 2010: 75–88.

Trinidad, A. "Wool and Keratin Research at the Eastern Regional Research Center." *Sheep Industry News* 16, 2012: 10–12.

Tucker P. "Bald Is Beautiful?: The Psychosocial Impact of Alopecia Areata." *Journal of Health Psychology* 14, 2009: 142–151.

Turing AM. "The Chemical Basis of Morphogenesis." *Philosophical Transactions of the Royal Society*, London B 237, 1952: 37–72.

van Beek N, Bodo E, Kromminga A, Gaspar E, et al. "Thyroid Hormones Directly Alter Human Hair Follicle Functions: Anagen Prolongation and Stimulation of Both Hair Matrix Keratinocyte Proliferation and Hair Pigmentation." *Journal of Clinical Endocrinology and Metabolism* 93, 2009: 4381–4388.

Van Clay M. "From Horse to Bow." *String Magazine*, January/February 1995.

Veldman MB, Zhao C, Gomez FA, et al. "Transdifferentiation of Fast Skeletal Muscle into Functional Endothelium In Vivo by Transcription Factor Etv2." *PLoS (Public Library of Science) Biol* 11, 2013: e1001590.

Vullo R, Girard V, Azar D, and Neraudeau D. "Mammalian Hairs in Early Cretaceous Amber." *Naturwissenschaften* 97, 2010: 683–687.

Wade N. *Before the Dawn: Recovering the Lost History of Our Ancestors.* New York: The Penguin Press, 2006.

Waites B. "Monasteries and the Wool Trade in North and East Yorkshire During the Thirteenth and Fourteenth Centuries." *Yorkshire Archeological Journal* 52, 1980:111–121.

Wang Y, Badea T, and Nathans J. "Order from Disorder: Self Organization in Mammalian Hair Patterning." *Proceedings of the National Academy of Sciences* 103, 2006: 19800–19805.

Weatherford, J. *Genghis Khan and the Making of the Modern World*. New York: Three Rivers Press, 2004.

Whitthoft J. "Archeology As a Key to the Colonial Fur Trade" in DL Morgan, et al. *Aspects of the Fur Trade: Selected Papers to the 1965 North American Fur Trade Conference*.St. Paul: Minnesota Historical Society, 1967: 55–61.

Zhang M, Brancaccio A, Weiner L, Missero C, and Brissette JL. "Ectodysplasin Regulates Pattern Formation in the Mammalian Hair Coat." *Genesis* 37, 2003: 30–37.

Zhang Y, Andl T, Yang SH, et al. "Activation of Beta-Catenin Signaling Programs Embryonic Epidermis to Hair Follicle Fate." *Development* 135, 2008: 2161–2175.

Zipes J. *The Complete Fairy Tales of the Brothers Grimm*. New York: Bantam Books, 1987.

NOTES

CHAPTER 1: THE FIRST FIBERS

1. Warren et al. "Genome Analysis of the Platypus Reveals Unique Signatures of Evolution." *Nature* 455, 2008: 256.
2. Dean I and Siva-Jothy MT. "Human Fine Body Hair Enhances Ectoparasite Detection." *Biology Letters* 8, 2012: 358–361.
3. Amoh Y, Li L, Katsuoka K, and Hoffman RM. "Multipotent Hair Follicle Stem Cells Promote Repair of Spinal Cord Injury and Recovery of Walking Function." *Cell Cycle* 7, 2008: 1865–1869.
4. Unlike other animals, mammals and birds have the ability to generate their own body heat aside from that generated by muscle activity. Because of this property, mammals and birds are considered endothermic (heated from the inside); moreover, because their body temperature is fairly constant (42°C for birds and 37°C for mammals), they are called homeothermic (constant body temperature). The turtle requiring sun to warm up is called ectothermic (heated from the outside) and, because its body temperature varies over the day, it is called poikilothermic (varying body temperature). Homeothermy is a major evolutionary gain because it gives animals some independence from daily and seasonal environmental temperature variations and opens most habitats to them.
5. Early mammals probably did feed on ectothermic dinosaurs. In a recent report, a triconodont mammal from the Lower Cretaceous of Liaoning, China, was found with a juvenile ceratopsian dinosaur in its stomach. Whether the mammal in this case was exploiting his endothermic advantage at the time was not clear.

Hu Y, Meng J, Wang Y, and Li C. "Large Mesozoic Mammals Fed on Young Dinosaurs." *Nature* 433, 2005: 149–152.

6. Ballantyne A. "Hypothermia: How Long Can Someone Survive in Frigid Water." *Scientific American*, January 16, 2009.

7. Conductive properties of materials: In W/moC conductivity of copper is 401, of wool/hair is 0.05, of water 0.58, of air 0.024. http://www.engineeringtoolbox .com/ thermal-conductivity-d_429.html.

8. Once humans lost their fur coat and acquired the ability to sweat, they could outrun the cheetah with a substantial head start; in fact, by these calculations one could imagine situations in which the overheated cheetah could now become prey to the naked sweaty ape.

9. Ruxton GD and Wilkinson DM. "Avoidance of Overheating and Selection for Both Hair Loss and Bipedality in Hominins." *Proceedings of the National Academy of Science* 108, 2011: 20965–20969.

10. Heat control is a major, complex, and fascinating element of animal biology and a driving force in evolution. Hair is only one aspect. Animals and humans have multiple means to adapt to different temperatures. There are reflexive ways of conserving heat, such as restricting blood flow to the extremities and gener- ating heat by shivering. There are also behavioral ways of conserving heat, such as reducing surface area by seeking shelter, by wearing clothes, by balling up, or by hugging your partner. There are also complex metabolic adaptive ways of keeping heat that involve special brown fat cells. Charles Darwin noted in his book *Voyage of the Beagle* (1845) that people can react to the same tempera- ture very differently. Darwin described local Indians in Tierra del Fuego who lived naked with just a shawl to blunt the harsh winter winds. In one scene, he describes "a small family of Fuegians, who were living in the cove, were quiet and inoffensive, and soon joined our party round a blazing fire. We were well clothed, and though sitting close to the fire were far from too warm; yet these naked savages, though further off, were observed, to our great surprise, to be streaming with perspiration at undergoing such a roasting." Darwin was observing adaptive thermogenesis, a process whereby the normal temperature set-point is slightly different, leading to striking differences in the ways groups of animals respond to ambient temperatures.

11. Explanations regarding family structure and monogamy are numerous. See PM Kappeler, "Why Male Mammals Are Monogamous." *Science* 341, 2013: 469–470.

12. One fascinatingly unique hair shaft is found on the African crested rat. Along its back, this animal has long, straight hair shafts that are perforated in such a way that the hairs can absorb large amounts of fluid. This rat slathers the mas- ticated toxin-laden root and bark of the *Acokanthera* tree onto the hairs, and the hairs rapidly wick up the poison, making them lethal. When threatened, the rat arches its back and points its hairs to the attacker. One taste of the poison-filled

hairs is able to sicken or even kill the attacker. The rat rapidly acquires a less-than-popular reputation among predators in the neighborhood.

13. Scientists who think a lot about hair suggest that there are hairs performing unusual functions in humans as well. Some are found in the underarm and groin. In these regions, the hair follicles are endowed with extra glands, the so-called apocrine glands, which empty their secretions into the upper follicle canal. Carried on the outgrowing hair shaft to the skin surface, these protein-rich secretions give rise to the distinctive whiff of a sweaty armpit. The apocrine secretions are considered to be one of the first signs of adolescence, as they are induced by sex hormones. Biologists have put forth an interesting (though largely unproven) notion suggesting that regional hair in humans—as in other mammals—can serve as an antenna to cast meaningful odors into the ambient environment. These secretions are asserted to belong to the group of odorous substances called pheromones, which are believed to provoke some sort of social action by the recipient, such as sexual attraction or orientation for proper mating (e.g., Desmond Morris, *The Naked Ape*). Though the claims are creative, logical, and widely espoused, the experiments in support of them are not yet convincing. In fact, the impact of armpit odor on human reproductive behavior could as easily be interpreted as repulsive as well as attractive.

CHAPTER 2: THE WAY THEY GROW

1. The ice cream analogy is illustrative of a gradient but in the description here it is simplified to the extreme. Recognize that in such a town setting the variables are legion, including people, traffic, sidewalks, weather, etc., which I did not control for in the example. It's overly simplistic, but I would hope the concept of a gradient, critical to modern ideas of pattern formation, will be grasped by most readers. I am indebted to Professor Lubert Stryer for this epicurean image.

2. Turing called the growth factors making up the gradient "morphogens," a word he coined that is derived from Greek roots (Gk, *morphe* shape; L. *generare*, produce) and means a substance that leads to the formation of shape. He envisioned that one cell would release a morphogen into the cell environment. The morphogen would spread away to form a gradient and then a distant cell would respond to that morphogen gradient by growing, ceasing to grow, beginning to migrate, changing shape, or even giving rise to a second morphogen in response to the gradient concentration at that point. In order for a stable pattern to develop, Turing found there had to be 1) positive and negative morphogens, 2) variable spread rate of different morphogens, where the inhibitor moves faster than the activator, and 3) the ability of morphogens to act back upon the cell that produced them, thus controlling their own production. Fundamental to his model is the processing of morphogens by the resident cells. Turing's paper took a very general approach to biological patterning and, though many other investigators have linked this paper to the patterning of hair follicles. Turing did

not mention hair follicles specifically. The Turing example illustrates current thought about pattern formation, but the reader must appreciate that the process is complex and still not fully understood.

3. Klar ARS. "Human Handedness and a Scalp Hair-Whorl Direction Develop from a Common Mechanism." *Genetics* 165, 2003: 269–276.

4. Weber B, Hoppe C, Faber J, Axmacher N, et al. "Association Between Scalp Hair-Whorl Direction and Hemispheric Language Dominance." *Neuroimage* 30, 2006: 539–543.

5. Murphy J and Arkins S. "Facial Hair Whorls (Trichoglyphs) and the Incidence of Motor Laterality in the Horse." *Behavioural Processes* 79, 2008: 7–12.

6. Tirosh E, Maffe M, and Dar H. "The Clinical Significance of Multiple Hair Whorls and Their Association with Unusual Dermatoglyphics and Dysmorphic Features in Mentally Retarded Israeli Children." *European Journal of Pediatrics* 146, 1987: 568–570.

7. Nowaczyk MJM and Sutcliff TL. "Blepharophimosis, Minor Facial Anomalies, Genital Anomalies, and Mental Retardation: Report of Two Sibs with a Unique Syndrome." *American Journal of Medical Genetics* 871, 1999: 78–81; Wilson GN, Richards CS, Katz K, and Brookshire GS. "Non-Specific X Linked Mental Retardation with Aphasia Exhibiting Genetic Linkage to Chromosomal Region Xp11." *Journal of Medical Genetics* 299, 1992: 629–634.

8. Le Douarin NM, Ziller C, Couly GF. "Patterning of Neural Crest Derivatives in the Avian Embryo: In Vivo and In Vitro Studies." *Developmental Biology* 159, 1993: 24–49.

CHAPTER 3: A MYSTERIOUS CYCLE AND A UNIQUE CELL

1. Dry FW. "The Coat of the Mouse (*Mus Musculus*)." *Journal of Genetics* 16, 1926: 281–340.

2. Most of our discussion concerning human hair follicles starts with the scalp; though other body follicles are very similar in structure and cycle, there are important differences from site to site, especially in the duration of cycle phases.

3. Hair follicle cells, like all cells, have rhythms, and the rhythms are set in part by the environment. But as cell life is based on chemistry, we have not addressed what molecules are beating the drum. It has been found, for example, that in most tissues there is a set of circadian clock genes, which turn on and off over the course of a day and affect the normal periods of sleep and activity. If these genes are disrupted, the affected mouse may sleep during the night while his normal brother is out foraging. In a laboratory setting, such aberrant behavior may not matter, but in the wild, a mouse gallivanting about during the day may provide an easily found, irresistible morsel to a predatory bird. Surprisingly, these same circadian clock genes are expressed in the hair follicle, and their concentration varies with the hair growth cycle. What is puzzling is that clock genes are associated with a circadian rhythm, while the hair cycle is decidedly

not circadian. So genes found to be important to twenty-four-hour cell growth processes in other systems appear to have been coopted by the hair follicle to control its own cycle ranging from days to years in duration. Researchers have shown that if these genes are not properly expressed in the hair follicle, follicle growth will be disrupted. How these genes influence hair follicle growth is not yet understood.

4. Hebert JM, Rosenquist T, Gotz J, and Martin GR. "FGF5 as a Regulator of the Hair Growth Cycle: Evidence from Targeted and Spontaneous Mutations." *Cell* 78, 1994: 1017–1025.

5. Higgins CA, Petukhova L, Harel S, et al. "FGF5 Is a Crucial Regulator of Hair Length in Humans." *Proceedings of the National Academy of Sciences* 111, 2014: 10648–10653.

6. Professor Colin Jahoda cautions that although most follicles cycle within "an internal developmental clock [for] many follicles it is extremely hard to determine what their developmental cycle is because there are so many other modulatory influences" (e-mail communication, CAB Jahoda, September 4, 2013).

7. While this statement is generally true, occasionally, after high-dose chemotherapy with various drug combinations such as cyclophosphamide, thiotepa, and carboplatin (CTC), some patients may experience irreversible hair loss.

8. Although earlier studies suggested that a common feature to all stem cells is their slow growth, Professor Hans Clever (*Development* 140, 2013: 2484–2489) and others have shown that there are subpopulations of cells with stem cell properties that grow rapidly and continuously.

9. Cotsarelis G, Sun TT, and Lavker, R. "Label-Retaining Cells Reside in the Bulge Area of Pilosebaceous Unit: Implications for Follicular Stem Cells, Hair Cycle, and Skin Carcinogenesis." *Cell* 61, 1990: 1329–1337.

10. Today we believe that dermal papilla factors act directly upon epidermal stem cells present in the various epidermal preparations Oliver, Jahoda, and others used to induce new hair follicles.

CHAPTER 4: INFLUENTIAL NEIGHBORS

1. Arck PC. E-mail communication. September 6, 2013; Arck PC, Handjiski B, Hagen E, Joachim R, Klapp BF, and Paus R. "Indications for a Brain–Hair Follicle Axis: Inhibition of Keratinocyte Proliferation and Up-Regulation of Keratinocytes Apoptosis in Telogen Hair Follicles by Stress and Substance P." *FASEB Journal* 15, 2001: 2536–2538; Arck PC, Handjiski B, Hagen E, Joachim R, Klapp BF, and Paus R. "Stress Inhibits Hair Growth in Mice by Induction of Premature Catagen Development and Deleterious Perifollicular Inflammation Events Via Neuropeptide Substance P-Dependent Pathways." *American Journal of Pathology* 162, 2003: 803–814.

2. In general, a normal adult does not produce new hair follicles. Follicle formation occurs once in human life and that is during the fetal stage of development.

However, a recent study (Ito M, Yang Z, Andl T, Cui C, Kim N, Millar SE, and Cotsarelis G. "Wnt-Dependent De Novo Hair Follicle Regeneration in Adult Mouse Skin After Wounding." *Nature* 447, 2007: 316–320) showed that in mice a major excision wound will repair with new hair follicles. This observation suggests that embedded in the repair process are the tools for organ regeneration. The phenomenon has not yet been shown to occur in humans.

3. Professor Paus and his group have presented data indicating that many of the circulating hormones made in endocrine organs are also made in the hair follicle itself and that the production of these hormones by the follicle is dependent on the hair-growth cycle. Although we are still learning how these homemade hormones act back on the hair follicles, we also ask the question if the hormones made by the hair follicle could affect the whole body. In this sense, could the tail wag the dog?

4. Major RH. *Classic Descriptions of Disease*. Third Edition. Springfield, IL: CC Thomas Publisher, 1965.

5. Patterned hair loss also occurs in women; it is common and devastating. I have not focused on this disorder because so much less is known about it than about male pattern balding. Its genetics, its androgen-dependence and its mechanism are uncertain. For the interested reader, I would recommend articles by A. Messenger (*Clinical Experimental Dermatology* 27, 2002: 383), P. Mirmirani (*Maturitas* 74, 2013: 119), and W. Bergfeld (*Dermatology Clinics* 31, 2013: 119).

6. Suetonius. *The Lives of the Twelve Caesars*, "On Julius Caesar." Translator J Gavorse. New York: Modern Library, 1959: 27.

7. Aristotle. *Generation of Animals*. Translator AL Peck. Cambridge: Harvard University Press, 1943: 525.

8. Hamilton J. "Male Hormone Is Prerequisite and an Incitant in Common Baldness." *American Journal of Anatomy* 71, 1942: 415–480.

9. Although the biological observations made by Hamilton are important to our understanding of the mechanism of male pattern balding, the modern reader cannot help but react with some uneasiness regarding the patient population he used. Interested in the legal and ethical attitudes regarding castration, I contacted the Connecticut state government. I am indebted to Mr. Lindsay Young, from the Law Unit of the Connecticut State Library, who assured me that there was no state law (at that time) prohibiting or permitting this practice. We assume that in the early part of the 20th century, castration had been a medically acceptable means for treating mental illness and delinquency. In my search of the literature and hair societies, I haven't been able to find where Hamilton found the group of castrated men he studied.

10. Hamilton JB. "Patterned Loss of Hair in Man; Types and Incidence." *Annals of the New York Academy of Sciences* 53, 1951: 708–728.

11. Developmental biologists have found that the skin and hair follicles from the top of the scalp and those from the side of the scalp are derived from different

embryonic tissues, one from somatic mesoderm and the other from neurocrestic mesoderm (Le Douarin NM, Ziller C, Couly GF. "Patterning of Neural Crest Derivatives in the Avian Embryo: In Vivo and In Vitro Studies." *Developmental Biology* 159, 1993: 24-49). That these two regions of the scalp come from different parts of the embryo is important because different embryonic regions give rise to tissues with very different properties.

CHAPTER 5: ENKIDU CUTS HIS HAIR

1.   Plummer W. *People Magazine*, August 11, 1997.
2.   Bickley C. E-mail communication. March 2, 2009.
3.   Most lay people refer to this disorder as "alopecia" but, in fact, "alopecia" in medical parlance refers to any condition of hair loss—and there are many. The problem in this disorder is that the body perceives the hair follicle as a type of *persona non grata*, an enemy to the sovereign state, and it musters an effective and unrelenting immune offensive on any follicle that dares appear. So in these otherwise healthy people, hair follicles start to grow normally, but they are cut down at a very early phase of growth. The wounded follicle abruptly ceases to grow before it can form a new shaft. Despite the insult, after a period of rest and repair, the hapless follicle tries, over and over again, with the same frustrated outcome. While we have some idea how the immune system may destroy hair follicle cells, we do not have the vaguest notion why. Cari Bickley is afflicted with the most severe form, while her husband, children, and close friends are not. Recent laboratory work indicates that this disorder has a genetic basis, as evidenced by familial and specific gene studies. Continuing to baffle us clinically, however, is that in many cases hair growth will return spontaneously—even in the severe form—without any obvious correlation to medical therapy, diet, living conditions, or emotional stress. This unpredictability poses a dilemma for the physician who must assess the efficacy of therapy: Did the aspirin actually work, or was the disease spontaneously regressing at the time the person was taking the aspirin? Unfortunately, since we don't have curative therapy today, the severely affected patient must learn to live without hair.
4.   McConnell TH. *The Nature of Disease: Pathology for the Health Professions*. Baltimore: Lippincott Williams and Wilkins, 2007: 655.
5.   In 1981, Professor Vera Price, a creative, farseeing, and doggedly persistent professor of dermatology at the University of California, San Francisco, and her colleague Vicky Kalabokes, a dynamic administrator, founded the National Alopecia Areata Foundation (www.naaf.org.), a patient support group established on the tenet that "the best therapy for someone who has alopecia areata is talking and interacting with others who have it." As such, the foundation offers hair-loss patients the opportunity to share personal experiences and to learn how others have coped.

6. West PM and Packer C. "Sexual Selection, Temperature, and the Lion's Mane." *Science* 297, 2007: 1339–1343.
7. Attitudes toward hair—like attitudes toward sex—are culturally and emotionally charged, and regarding hair, no one wants to be told he or she is losing it. If the subject arises in conversation, the targeted person receives the comment with embarrassed, if not resentful, humor. Moreover, hair in human society services a visual image, not a tactile one. Accordingly, to touch another person's hair without well-defined permission is taboo in virtually all cultures.
8. Christoforou, C. *Whose Hair?* London: Laurence King Publishing, 2011: 3.
9. Hairstyles of people living in highly traditional cultures tend to last longer; their hair fashions cycle but at a slower pace.
10. Sherrow V. *Encyclopedia of Hair: A Cultural History.* Westport, CT: Greenwood Press, 2006: 300.
11. Basler RP. *Abraham Lincoln: His Speeches and Writings.* Cleveland, OH: World Publishing Company, 1946: 561.
12. Sears JR. "The Sane View of Anthony Wayne." *Harper's Magazine* 105, 1902: 886.
13. Silverman RE. "Bald Is Beautiful. A Buzzed Head Can Be Masculine, a Touch Aggressive and, as a New Study Suggests, an Advantage in Business." *Wall Street Journal,* October 3, 2012.
14. Sherrow V. *Encyclopedia of Hair: A Cultural History.* Westport, CT: Greenwood Press, 2006: 191.
15. Cutler WP, Cutler JP, Dawes EC, and Force P. *Life, Journal and Correspondence of Rev Manasseh Cutler, LLD.* Cincinnati, OH:.Robert Clarke and Company, 1888: 231.
16. Mitchell A., translator. *Gilgamesh: A New English Version.* New York: Simon & Schuster, 2004.
17. Since the Latin word for beard is *barba*, one might surmise that the Romans based their word for foreignness on their enemies' hirsute display. However, the word "barbarian" probably derives from a Greek root referring to a foreigner, or a person who does not speak the common language, nothing to do with hair (Oxford English Dictionary). In any case, from wherever the word came, most societies, including these, interpreted long, unruly hair as a sign of people who were wild, uncivilized, untrustworthy, unpredictable, threatening, and just plain distasteful.
18. http://www.jewishgen.org/ForgottenCamps/Camps/AuschwitzEng.html.
19. Tharps LL. "Black Hair and Identity Politics" in A. Bell. *Hair.* Newark, NJ: Rutgers University, 2013: 24–26.
20. The tools of hair care in general have also been perceived to have sexual associations. The term a "jeweled comb box" is used poetically in Japan to refer to both sexual secrets and female genitals. "To open one's comb box," for instance, metaphorically describes a woman's giving her body to a man. The important trope

in this reference is "comb," linking hair to the message. As combs control hair, they symbolically perform the same role that cultural mores play on natural sexual drives. Hair that is well combed and securely placed suggests sexual discipline and self-control, though a creative suitor might see that tied-up hair can also be let down again. As a young woman, Queen Victoria of England kept her hair in a tight bun in public but let it down in the privacy of her home, bequeathing to Great Britain and the world nine children who sat on many European thrones.

21. The Freudians take the sexual message of hair to the extreme. In some renditions, their concept of hair is entirely sexual. For them, man's functions on earth—at least his animal functions—are eating, sleeping in security, and then procreating. As the Freudians see it, since most of the time is spent trying to mate or actually mating, the small things in life take on sexual symbolism. For example, scalp hair represents the whole sexual experience, with scalp hairs embodying an elaboration of pubic hair and individual hairs becoming phallic symbols (Berg C. *The Unconscious Significance of Hair*. Leicester: Black Friars Press Ltd, 1951).

22. Although it remains to be seen how long and widespread the practice of man-scaping will be, there is no doubt many men today prefer to be as hairless as many women.

23. Sherrow V. *Encyclopedia of Hair: A Cultural History*. Westport, CT: Greenwood Press, 2006: 315; and Alexander B. "Personal Grooming Down There." 2005. MNSBC News, http://www.nbcnews.com/id/4751816#.Va_TSqPD9D8.

24. Allison A. "Cutting the Fringes: Pubic Hair at the Margins of Japanese Censorship Laws." in *Hair: Its Power and Meaning in Asian Cultures*. Editors A Hiltebeitel and BD Miller. Albany: State University of New York Press, 1998.

25. International Society of Hair Restoration Surgery report of 2015 states that pubic transplants make up 0.2 percent of the number of hair transplant procedures and 85 percent of that number occurs in Asia, illustrating a cultural value.

26. Ibid.

27. Thompson JJ. "Cuts and Culture in Kathmandu" in *Hair: Its Power and Meaning in Asian Cultures*. Editors A Hiltebeitel and BD Miller. Albany: State University of New York Press, 1998.

28. Jordan M. "Hair Matters in South Central Africa" in *Hair in African Art and Culture*. Editors R Sieber and F Herreman. New York: Museum for African Art, 2000.

29. I am indebted to Arben Nace for this reference.

30. Bacuez L. *Priestly Vocation and Tonsure*. New York: Imprimatur John M Farley, Archbishop of New York, 1908.

CHAPTER 6: BARBERS AND BEAUTICIANS

1. Dobson J and Walker RM. *Barbers and Barber-Surgeons of London: A History of the Barbers' and Barber-Surgeons' Company*. Oxford: Blackwell Scientific Publishers, 1979.

2. In Rome at the time of Christ, craftsmen, called *tonsores* (from the Latin *tonsorius*—shaving), shaved beards, cut hair, drew teeth, and let blood. The practice of bloodletting was based on the idea that blood, one of the cardinal body humors, went out of balance in disease and could be brought back to normal by bleeding. The first record of bloodletting occurs on a Greek vase dating from 500 B.C.E.. It became progressively more important after it was championed by the popular Greek physician Galen (129–200 C.E.). This ill-conceived procedure died out in the late 18th century.

3. In the Middle Ages, a guild was a trade organization, or brotherhood, invested by the government, and consisting of people of special skills. Established by Edward the Confessor around 1066, the first recorded guild in England was composed of young noblemen who were obliged to carry out three combats at Smithfield before the king. From this time onward, the guilds served to control a trade and to provide the royal treasury with monies when needed. A craftsman could not practice his art without the blessing of the trade guild; moreover, in the reign of Edward II, no person, whether an inhabitant of the City or not, was admitted to civic freedom unless he was a member of a guild. Guild members had complete control over the trade of their craft: price, market, product standards, membership, and training. Each guild might have its own priests and distinctive livery. In return for this great power, the guilds were indebted to the king and they supplied him liberally with funds when requested—such as the £5,000 Edward II demanded from the City Companies in 1340 to help defray his campaigns in the Hundred Years' War. By the 13th century, there were numerous guilds in London including those for the saddlers, cloth weavers, goldsmiths, tailors, and bakers.

4. Robinson JO. "The Barber-Surgeons of London." *Archives of Surgery* 119, 1988: 1171–1175.

5. Today, the turf battle between barber and surgeon lingers. Hair transplantation and facial reconstructions are the exclusive domain of plastic surgeons, but non-surgeons compete with surgeons for minimally invasive procedures such as tattoo construction or removal, Botox injections, facial peels, and laser skin treatments. The dividing line between beauty and medical procedures remains a point of conflict and tightening regulation (e.g., Beck M. "Medical Spas Get a Checkup: States Weigh Tighter Rules on Cosmetic-Procedure Centers After Patient Injuries." *Wall Street Journal*, June 5, 2013: A3). Although safety is the primary issue here, the business considerations between these two groups are reminiscent of the barber-surgeon conflicts of the 18th century.

6. Opportunities for anatomic dissection exemplify the important difference in training between the two groups. The bodies of four prisoners, who had been "condemned, adjudged and put to death for felony by the due order of the King's law," were offered to each surgeon for anatomic dissection.

Barber-surgeons did not enjoy this privilege. (Dobson J and Walker RM. *Barbers and Barber-Surgeons of London: A History of the Barbers' and Barber-Surgeons' Company*. Oxford: Blackwell Scientific Publishers, 1979: 34; and Jutte R. "A Seventeenth-Century German Barber-Surgeon and His Patients." *Medical History* 33, 1989: 184–198.)

7. Cox JS. *An Illustrated Dictionary of Hairdressing and Wigmaking*. London: BT Batsford, 1989.

8. Abel AL. "Blood Letting: Barber-Surgeons' Shaving and Bleeding Bowls." *Journal of the American Medical Association* 214, 1970: 900–901.

9. Pennsylvania Code 2011:3.45, Commonwealth of Pennsylvania. Title 49. Professional and Vocational Standards. Chapter 3. State Board of Barber Examiners. January 8, 2011.

10. Bristol DW. *Knights of the Razor: Black Barbers in Slavery and Freedom*. Baltimore: The Johns Hopkins University Press, 2009.

11. Ibid.

12. Ibid.

13. There are three extant barbershop-style singing societies: for men, the Barbershop Harmony Society, and for women, Sweet Adeline International and Harmony Incorporated. They have regular meetings and are open to new members who enjoy singing.

14. Stanley J. "The Life of Benjamin Franklin; with Selections from His Miscellaneous Works." London: Simpkin, Marshall and Co, 1849: 55.

15. Sherrow V. *Encyclopedia of Hair: A Cultural History*. Westport: Greenwood Press, 2006.

CHAPTER 7: THE HAIR-HANG ACT

1. Hair shaft strength is due to its cortex, a thick, dense, cylindrical layer constituting the fiber middle. Like the stem of a tree, the cortex is made of tightly packed, spindle-shaped cells, firmly attached to one another and stretching along the vertical axis. In both structures, the cells are made of regularly packed filaments in an amorphous matrix, molecular glue. In nature, such composite materials, made of filaments plus matrix, manifest extraordinary strength that either component alone would not have: Filaments provide rigidity and the embedded matrix resistance to compression. In reinforced concrete, iron rods make up the filaments and concrete the matrix; for wood, cellulose fibers make up the filaments and lignin the matrix; for hair, keratin proteins make up the filaments and keratin-associated proteins, the glue, make up the matrix. While the mechanical theme between these three materials is common, the constituent molecules are very different: complex inorganic molecules versus complex carbohydrates versus complex proteins. It is the two-component composite structure of the hair shaft that allows a "hair-hang" to occur.

2. Bomont P, et al. "The Gene Encoding Gigaxonin, a New Member of the Cyto-skeletal BRB/Kelch Repeat Family, Is Mutated in Giant Axonal Neuropathy." *Nature Genetics* 26, 2000: 370–374.

3. Clack AA, Macphee RD, and Poinar HN. "Case Study: Ancient Sloth DNA Recovered from Hairs Preserved in Paleofeces." *Methods in Molecular Biology* 840, 2012: 51–56.

4. Koc O, Yildiz, FD, Narci A, and Sen TA. "An Unusual Cause of Gastric Per-foration in Childhood: Trichobezoar (Rapunzel Syndrome). A Case Report." *European Journal of Pediatrics* 168, 2009: 495–497.

5. Please recall that although wool is a natural fiber, it is also hair.

6. Unaware pets have had lethal exposures to quills. Johnson MD, Magnusson KD, Shmon CL, and Waldner C. "Porcupine Quill Injuries in Dogs: A Ret-rospective of 296 Cases (1998–2002)." *Canadian Veterinary Journal* 47, 2007: 677–682.

7. Laufer B. "The Early History of Felt." *American Anthropologist, New Series* 32, 1930: 4.

CHAPTER 8: COMB, SCISSORS, CURLER, DYE

1. Sankararanaman S et al. "The Genomic Landscape of Neanderthal Ancestry in Present Day Humans." *Nature* 507, 2014: 354-357.

2. Nagase S, Tsuchiya M, Matsui T, Shibuichi S, et al. "Characterization of Curved Hair of Japanese Women with Reference to Internal Structures and Amino Acid Composition." *Journal of Cosmetic Science* 59, 2008: 317–332.

3. Hair density is lowest among Asians compared to Africans and Europeans, but it grows faster in Asians.

4. Khumalo NP. "Yes, Let's Abandon Race—It Does Not Accurately Corre-late with Hair Form." *Journal of the American Academy of Dermatology* 56, 2007: 709–710.

5. De la Mettrie R, Saint-Leger D, Loussouarn G, Garcel A, Porter C, and Lan-ganey A. "Shape Variability and Classification of Human Hair: A Worldwide Approach." *Human Biology* 79, 2007: 265–281.

6. Khumalo NP. Ibid.

7. It takes a lot of injury to strip the cuticle from the human shaft because the cuticle is multilayered, consisting of ten overlapping cells like tiles on a roof: For every upward-pointing cuticle cell on the shaft surface, there are about ten cells underlying it.

8. Living cells make up the hair shaft base, but once these cells leave the base they solidify and die. The hair shaft is essentially a tightly held collection of fossilized cells.

9. Robbins CR. *Chemical and Physical Behavior of Human Hair.* New York: Springer-Verlag, 2002.

10. Ibid.

11. The global market for all hair products is estimated to be $58 billion in 2015 with market for hair dyes about $10 billion. I am indebted to John Gray (Proctor and Gamble Co.) for this estimate.

12. Bryer R. *The History of Hair: Fashion and Fantasy Down the Ages*. London: Philip Wilson Publishers, 2005.

13. There is a spectrum of hair color permanence that is dependent on the chemicals and procedure used, resulting in temporary, semi-permanent, demi-permanent, or permanent color. We only consider the extremes in this chapter.

14. The forensic investigator recognizes that while the cuticle of dyed hair is pigmented, the cuticle of natural hair is not.

CHAPTER 9: THE ULTIMATE ARTIFICE

1. Dorfman C. Wigmaker, Saint Paul, MN. Telephone interview. September 4, 2012.

2. Though the morbid thought may make the start of a good mystery, I have been assured that in no instance does modern wig hair come from dead people (Mawbey R. Personal interview. London, October 15, 2012; Ruskai M & Lowery A, 2010).

3. Rai, S. "A Religious Tangle over the Hair of Pious Hindus. " *The New York Times*, July 14, 2004.

4. I am indebted to M. Minowa for hosting this visit (November 2011).

5. Ruskai M and Lowery A. *Wig Making and Styling*. Amsterdam: Elsevier, 2010: 54–55.

6. Minowa, M. Aderans Ltd, Tokyo. E-mail letter of personal interview. August 10, 2015.

CHAPTER 10: QUEEN VICTORIA'S MEMENTO

1. Lacy M. "Lone Bidder Buys Strands of Che's Hair at U.S. Auction." *The New York Times International Edition*, October 26, 2007.

2. Sieber R and Herreman F. *Hair in African Art and Culture*. New York: Museum for African Art, 2000.

3. Esmi, R. *A Connecticut Family*. Master's Thesis. Middletown: Wesleyan University, 1996.

4. Tait, H., editor. *Jewelry: 7000 Years*. New York: Harry N. Abrams Inc., 1986.

5. Tuite C. "Tainted Love and Romantic Literary Celebrity." *English Literary History* 74, 2007: 59–88.

6. Esmi, R. *A Connecticut Family*. Master's Thesis. Middletown: Wesleyan University, 1996.

7. Cohoon, Leila. Leila Cohoon Museum. Personal interview. February 23, 2013.

8. Holden C. "Comment" in Bell A. *Hair*. Newark: Rutgers University, 2013: 78.

9. Human hair may serve as an art medium whether it is cut off and displayed in formal artworks or still growing on the scalp. In fact, elaborate hair designs

have been appreciated in most cultures for their artistic value. While Western cultures have a rich tradition of unique and attractive hair arrangements, perhaps the most elaborate hair designs in existence today appear among men and women of sub-Saharan Africa, where the hairstyles are complex, involving braiding, bundling, and trimming with added embellishments, such as wigs, plant material, and jewelry. These hairdos take exceptional artistic skill and a good deal of time to compose. Reference to hair appears in most art forms, including jewelry, graphics or sculpture, poetry, literature, dance, and every kind of music. In this chapter, we restrict examples to jewelry and sculpture.

CHAPTER 11: QUEST FOR BEAVER MAPS A CONTINENT

1. The exact time when humans first started to wear skins is uncertain, though recent gene sequencing work suggests a possible start. This approximation is based on the notion that humans first put on clothing about the time human body lice (*Pediculis hominus*) appeared. The argument has four points. First, lice are very fussy animals; in fact, they cannot live off the warm human body longer than a few hours. Second, the head louse is ensconced on the scalp because that's the only place on the human body it comfortably exists (similarly, the pubic louse is restricted to the groin). Third, though all lice living on humans are undoubtedly related, as determined by genome sequencing, the scalp louse is phylogenetically older and very likely the progenitor of the body louse. Finally, humans lost their dense body hair long before the body louse made its appearance, so the evolving body louse had to adapt to life on somebody else's hair. Based on these observations and genetic timing, the argument goes, head lice evolved into body lice on the human's newly expropriated body hair, fur clothing, no later than seventy-two thousand years ago. By this line of evidence, then, humans have been clothing their bodies for roughly one hundred thousand years.

2. Notably Pepys paid four pounds, five shillings for his hat and he earned about £350 per year. Wheatley HB, editor. *Diary of Samuel Pepys*. New York: Random House, 1893: 27 June 1661.

3. Phillips PC. *The Fur Trade: Volume 1*. Norman: University of Oklahoma Press, 1961.

4. Whitthoft J. "Archeology as a Key to the Colonial Fur Trade." In Morgan et al. *Aspects of the Fur Trade. Selected Papers to the 1965 North American Fur Trade Conference*. St Paul: Minnesota Historical Society, 1967: 55–61.

5. Evidence that the Indians were savvy regarding the white man comes from very early records. In 1534, Cartier found on the shore of the Gaspe Peninsula a group of natives who wanted to trade; he notes "they made all the young women retire" before the trade commenced, suggesting the Indians knew even at this early time to be wary of European sailors (Eccles WJ. *The Canadian Frontier 1534–1760*. Albuquerque: University of New Mexico Press, 1983: 13).

6. Alan Herscovici, Personal interview. Montreal, May 2009; phone interview February 25, 2014; Herscovici A. *Second Nature: The Animal-Rights Controversy.* Montreal: CBC Enterprises, 1985.

7. *International Fur Trade Federation*, www.wearefur.com.

CHAPTER 12: WOOL BANKROLLS AN EMPIRE

1. Leggett WF. *The Story of Wool.* Brooklyn: Chemical Publishing Company, 1947.

2. Ibid.

3. Depending on the time and place, the weight of one wool sack varied; however, we know that in 1337 William de la Pole sold sacks weighing 364 pounds each (Fryde EB. *The Wool Accounts of William de la Pole: A Study of Some Aspects of the English Wool Trade at the Start of the Hundred Years' War.* York: St Anthony's Press, 1964). At other times, a sack weighed much less.

4. Leggett WF. Ibid.

5. In 1273, English merchants controlled only 30 percent of the home wool export trade. Slowly, English merchants and banks took over this function, so that by the 15th century, home banks controlled more than 80 percent of it. This change from foreign- to domestic-owned banking reflected a change in how the English were using their home-grown wool (Lockett A. *Wool Trade.* London: Methuen Educational Ltd, 1974).

6. Powers E. *The Wool Trade in English Medieval History.* Oxford: Oxford University Press, 1941.

7. The "Burial in Woollen Acts" of 1666 (http://www.british-history.ac.uk/report.asp?compid=47386).

8. Leggett WF. *The Story of Wool.* Brooklyn: Chemical Publishing Company, 1947.

9. Origo, Iris. *The Merchant of Prato: Francesco Di Marco Datini, 1335–1410.* New York: Alfred A. Knopf, 1957: 35.

10. Ref. http://www.parliament.uk/site-information/glossary/woolsack/.

11. Powers E. *The Wool Trade in English Medieval History.* Oxford: Oxford University Press, 1941.

12. Ref. http://www.northleach.org/history/wool/.

13. Modern shepherds are hardly better off; the life is hard and poorly paid, as illustrated by a recent report by the *New York Times*. The shepherd interviewed was Cortez Vargas, one of fifteen hundred sheepherders working in the United States. He drives a flock of two thousand sheep across the Rocky Mountains in Wyoming and Colorado; ranchers pay him $750 a month for working around the clock without a day off. He lives in a five-by-ten-foot trailer without running water. Ranchers argue that in the low-margin industry of wool production they cannot afford to pay more. A lawyer for the Colorado Legal Services, Jennifer Lee, describes the life of the shepherd as the "modern day form of indentured servitude" (Frosch D. "A Lonely and Bleak Existence in the West, Tending the Flock." *The New York Times*, February 22, 2009). Recent directives

by the U.S. Labor Department raising the minimal wages for shepherds may address some of these issues (*New York Times,* October 14, 2015).

14. Power E. *The Wool Trade in English Medieval History.* Oxford: Oxford University Press, 1941.

15. Biotechnologists have entered wool shearing. Australian scientists found that one skin injection of a small protein called epidermal growth factor will cause fleece to shed (Moore GP, Panaretto BA, Robertson D. "Inhibition of Wool Growth in Merino Sheep Following Administration of Mouse Epidermal Growth Factor and a Derivative." *Australian Journal of Biological Science* 35, 1982: 163–72; and *Bioclip Editorial Science* 281, 1998: 511). This growth factor blocks growth of the cells at the bottom of the hair shaft, which weakens shaft structure at that point. In two weeks the shaft breaks, the fleece drops off, leaving the sheep "sheared." The advantage of molecular de-fleecing is that it is fast, easy, efficient, clean, and without skin cuts.

16. Both beaver and sheep fur have an overfur layer made of strong, long, straight hairs and an underfur layer made of short, thin, curled hairs. Fleece of sheep is similar to fur of the beaver, though the character of the fur differs, and this difference defines its use. The beaver's short, soft underfur is optimal for felting and hat-making; for the weaver, the longer fibers of fine sheep wool are essential.

17. While in the heyday of the medieval wool trade, the choice sheep were English, by the late 18th century, a super-breed from Spain—the merino—became available. The merino sheep probably arose from an ancestor brought by Arab traders to Spain from Syria and Arabia in the 7th century. In Spain, these sheep were bred with other wool-producing sheep, including the fine English breeds. Merino sheep were recognized for their fine wool as early as the 13th and 14th centuries, but because the Spanish king put an embargo on their trade, neither sheep nor fleece entered the larger European market. Not until the reign of George III in the late 1700s did merino sheep enter England. Since that time, breeders have introduced merino sheep to all parts of the world. In Australia and New Zealand, the merino sheep flourished to spawn a massive wool industry in the early 19th century. This breed is choice because it produces a wool-rich fleece: Its fibers are very fine, curled, and long, a result of an unusually long anagen phase of the sheep's hair growth cycle. Merinos' wool shaft diameter is very thin, ranging in thickness from two to six red blood cells; such a width is barely visible. The degree of crimp is described by the length of the naturally curled fiber to the length of the same fiber stretched. For fine merino wool, the crimped fiber measures one-and-one-half to three inches and the stretched fiber measures ten inches; coarse-haired wool, on the other hand, might have an equal fiber length if relaxed or stretched. Today, woolworkers consider the merino the most valuable wool sheep ever bred.

18. Jenkins JG, editor. *The Textile Industry in Great Britain*. London: Routledge & Kegan Paul, 1972: 85.

19. Broudy E. *The Book of Looms: History of the Handloom from Ancient Times to the Present*. Hanover: Brown University Press, 1979.

20. Cultural anthropologists assume the first use of wool for cloth was in the form of felt because it is easy to make: Collect wool, clean it, wet it, heat it, and press it. Uncertainty in the date of first wool use and weaving could be due to the fact that hair is not stable in wet, warm conditions. Evidence suggests that humans were weaving plant fibers before animal hair. In 2009, Harvard archeologist Ofer Bar-Yosef reported that peoples living in the Caucasus Mountains about the time modern humans migrated into the area from Africa, dating as early as thirty-six thousand years ago, were weaving flax fiber (Kvavadze et al. "30,000 Year Old Flax Fibers." *Science* 328, 2009: 1634). At the same site, the team found a few twisted and colored fibers of goat wool. The earliest spun and woven wool dates to about twelve thousand years ago in northern Europe and the oldest loom to roughly 5000 B.C.E.

21. Though weaving can be performed—albeit slowly and inefficiently—without a heddle (a device that separates warp fibers and thus spares the weaver the task of lifting each warp fiber to thread the weft fiber) archeologists contend that the heddle is indispensable to the authentic loom.

22. LE Fisher. *The Weavers*. New York: Franklin Watts Publishing, 1966.

23. www.cirfs.org

24. www.Sheep101.info

25. Food and Agriculture organization of the United Nations, http://www.fao.org/agriculture/lead/themes0/climate/en/.

26. Binkley C. "Which Outfit Is Greenest? A New Rating Tool." *Wall Street Journal*, July 12, 2012.

CHAPTER 13: BEYOND CLOTHES

1. Ballard, Lance. Sherwin-Williams Company. Telephone interview. July 25, 2013.

2. Walton I and Cotton C. *The Compleat Angler 1653*. Oxford: Oxford University Press, 1982.

3. To serve its bouncing function, the tennis ball had to be made of the most elastic material available at the time. Compare the elastic modulus of modern rubber of 0.1 (which they did not have) to steel 200, wood or sawdust 11, flax 58, and wool 3.4. So it was reasonable to pack wool or hair into a ball that needed a bounce.

4. Flynn, Sean. Wilson Sporting Goods. Telephone interview. April 15, 2013.

5. Knutson R. "Recession Puts a Kink in Operation That Uses Locks to Soak Up Oil Spills." *Wall Street Journal*, August 10, 2009.

6. Currently there are synthetic products available that have oil-absorbent properties. For example, the firm PIG (in Tipton, Pennsylvania) makes absorbent pads

and sausages to collect fluid spills. Different absorbents are used for different materials. Those sausages containing polypropylenes are used for oil spills. Although they have not used hair in their product, members of the sales force thought hair could be a cheaper option if there were an efficient collection system (Public Relations Dept., PIG Co., August 30, 2013).

7. Nicas J. "Flawed Evidence Under a Microscope." *Wall Street Journal*, July 19, 2013.

8. Alexander KL. "DNA Test Set Free D.C. Man Held in Student's 1981 Slaying." *Washington Post*, December 16, 2009.

9. http://murderpedia.org/female.L/l/li-tianle.htm.

10. Office of the State Medical Examiner, New Jersey. September 8, 2015.

11. The DNA captured from hair may arise from either the nucleus or the mitochondria. In early studies, scientists could isolate only mitochondrial DNA. Because mitochondria are mother-derived, the information conveyed from this DNA only reflects the maternal line. Recently, methods for extracting nuclear or genomic DNA from hair have made hair the ideal source of DNA. One set of researchers (Rasmussen M, Li Y, Lindgren S, et al. "Ancient Human Genome Sequence of an Extinct Palaeo-Eskimo." *Nature* 463, 2010: 757–762) recovered informative DNA using a tuft of hair from a four-thousand-year-old human preserved in the Greenland permafrost. The advantage of hair is that recoverable DNA is not on the surface but inside the shaft (Gilbert MT, Tomsho LP, Rendulic S, et al. "Whole-Genome Shotgun Sequencing of Mitochondria from Ancient Hair Shafts." *Science* 317, 2007: 1927–1930) so the shaft can be washed of irrelevant DNA without losing native DNA. Other tissues, such as muscle or bone, cannot be cleaned as well and thus are often contaminated with genetic material from other sources, such as bacteria.

12. Swardson A. "A Telltale Heart Finds Its Place in History." *Washington Post Foreign Service*, April 20, 2000.

13. Kintz P. "Bioanalytical Procedures for Detection of Chemical Agents in Hair in the Case of Drug-Facilitated Crimes." *Analytical and Bioanalytical Chemistry* 388, 2007: 1467–1474.

14. Rashed MN and Soltan ME. "Animal Hair as Biological Indicator for Heavy Metal Pollution in Urban and Rural Areas." *Environmental Monitoring and Assessment* 110, 2005: 41–53.

15. Cooper GAA, Kronstrand R, and Kintz P. "Society of Hair Testing Guidelines for Drug Testing in Hair." *Forensic Science International* 218, 2012: 20–24.

16. Lin X, Alber D, Henkelmann R. "Elemental Contents in Napoleon's Hair Cut Before and After His Death: Did Napoleon Die of Arsenic Poisoning?" *Analytical and Bioanalytical Chemistry* 379, 2004: 218–220.

17. According to Hank Engster from Perdue Chicken, Maryland (Perdue Chicken Co. Telephone interview. 2013), chicken feed is 85 percent protein, mostly provided by soybeans but a minor contribution from feathers (2 percent).

Feather meal is inexpensive and superior to soybean meal in terms of total cysteine, valine, and threonine content. While the most common method of releasing feather protein is by heat, industrialists also use bacterial keratinases (Deivasigamani B. "Industrial Application of Keratinase and Soluble Proteins from Feather Keratins." *Journal of Environmental Biology* 29, 2008: 933). Breaking down feather or hair by fermentation is gentler than by heat, resulting in higher concentrations of the essential amino acids methionine, lysine, and arginine (Gupta R and Ramnani P. "Microbial Keratinases and Their Prospective Applications: An Overview." *Applied Microbiology and Biotechnology* 70, 2006: 21–33).

18. Jizhou Huaheng Bio and Tech Co. Ltd. makes a highly purified cysteine (AJ192 grade) from human hair, which is exported and used in human foodstuffs.

EPILOGUE: A GLIMPSE OF THE FUTURE

1. Twain, Mark. "About Barbers" in *Sketches New and Old (Complete)*. Teddington, UK: The Echo Library, 1875.

2. In composing this futuristic chapter I spoke with some of the most noted thinkers in the field of modern hair biology and clinical medicine: professors Rox Anderson (Harvard University, November 21, 2013; telephone); Cheung Ming Chuong (University of Southern California, December 9, 2013; telephone); George Cotsarelis (University of Pennsylvania, October 30, 2013; personal interview); Elaine Fuchs (Rockefeller University, November 1, 2013; personal interview), Paradi Mirmirani (Kaiser Permanente, October 9, 2013; telephone); Ralf Paus (Manchester University, October 10, 2013; telephone); Vera Price (University of California, San Francisco, November 21, 2013; telephone); Jerry Shapiro (University of British Columbia, October 8, 2013; telephone), Desmond Tobin (University of Bradford, December 6, 2013; telephone); Annika Vogt (Charite University, December 13, 2013; telephone); Ken Washenik (Bosley Medical Group, New York City, September 27, 2013; personal interview); Mr. Charles Kirkpatrick (National Association of Barber Boards, September 25, 2013; telephone); Mike Ippoliti (National Barber Museum, September 24, 2013; telephone).

   The ideas expressed make up an amalgam of projections they shared with me. I am most indebted to this group for their time and flight-of-fancy thoughts.

3. Alfred Natrasevschi. Telephone interview. November 11, 2013.

4. Because the follicles transplanted to the top of the head are hardwired to believe they are living on the side of the scalp, they will continue to grow in the bald spot looking like side-of-scalp hair. The principle of donor dominance is true for any transplanted follicle and the principle can be a problem for the cosmetic surgeon. When women need transplanted hair for lost eyebrows, the surgeon usually uses scalp follicles (which have a long anagen growth phase) because those are the only follicles available. The patient with the newly transplanted

scalp follicles in the eyebrow region achieves the desired look but is forced to trim her new eyebrows regularly.

5. Orentreich N. "Autografts in Alopecias and Other Selected Dermatological Conditions." *Annals of the New York Academy of Sciences* 83, 1959: 463–79.
6. Dr. Kenneth Washenik, Bosley Medical Group. Personal interview. New York City, September 27, 2013.
7. International Society of Hair Restoration Surgeons; 2015 Practice Census Results; www.ishrs.org.
8. Canales, M. Restoration Robotics. Phone interview. November 14, 2013.
9. The growth factors that Yamanaka and his team placed into fibroblasts to make stem cells are presented here by the acronym SOKM: Sox 2, Oct 3/4, Klf 4, and c-Myc. (Takashi K and Yamanaka S. "Induction of Pluripotent Stem Cells from Mouse Embryonic and Adult Fibroblast Cultures by Defined Factors." *Cell* 126, 2006: 663–676.)
10. He J, Lu H, et al. "Regeneration of Liver After Extreme Hepatocyte Loss Occurs Mainly Via Biliary Transdifferentiation in Zebra Fish." *Gastroenterology* 146, 2013: 789–800.
11. Inagawa K, Ieda M. "Direct Reprogramming of Mouse Fibroblasts into Cardiac Myocytes." *Journal of Cardiovascular Translational Research* 6, 2013: 37–45.
12. Veldman MB, Zhao C, Gomez FA, et al. "Transdifferentiation of Fast Skeletal Muscle into Functional Endothelium In Vivo by Transcription Facto Etv2." PLoS (Public Library of Science) *Biology* 11, 2013: e1001590.

INDEX

H

hair. *See also* hair follicles; hair shafts
  in art, 114–117, 148–149
  beauty and, 51–55
  brain and, 24–25
  chemical record of, 157–159
  collecting, 111–117
  color of, 39–40, 55, 93–96
  combing, 90–91
  cowlicks, 24, 108
  durability of, 80–84
  environmental uses of, 152
  from famous people, 111–117
  first haircut, 68–69
  in food industry, 159–160
  in forensics, 152–155, 157–158
  future of, 161–169
  gray hair, 55, 94–95
  growth cycle of, 26–38
  growth pattern of, 16–25, 163–164
  healthy hair, 46–47, 63–64, 81–83, 105
  in jewelry, 112–117
  as keepsake, 112–117
  life history of, 157
  loss of, 12–14, 24–34, 37, 40–47, 52–53,
      63–64, 101–102
  as memento, 112–117
  messages sent by, 51–70
  music and, 41–42, 149–151
  origin of, 5–8
  patterning of, 16–25
  as sensory device, 8–10
  shedding, 29–34, 40–41, 63
  sound and, 41–42
  in sporting goods, 151–152
  strength of, 80–82
  styling, 90–93
  for temperature control, 9–13
  transplanting, 163–166
  types of, 18, 89–90, 154
  uses of, 147–160
  for visual arts, 148–149
  whorls, 24, 108
hair color, 39–40, 55, 93–96
hair conditioners, 91
hair cuticle, 85

hair cycle, 26–38
hair dyes, 95–96
hair fibers, 3–4, 147–160
hair follicles. *See also* hair shafts
  anagen growth phase of, 29–37, 41–42, 94
  arrangement of, 16–18
  catagen phase of, 30–31, 41
  cycle of, 26–38
  exogen phase of, 31–32
  formation of, 5–8, 18–23, 82, 157
  mature follicles, 5
  structure of, 4, 29
  study of, 26–28
  telogen phase of, 31, 33–34, 42
  transplanting, 163–166
hair growth, 16–38, 163–164
"hair hanging" act, 80–82
hair jewelry, 112–117
hair permanents, 93
hair removal, 64, 69, 168–169
hair salons, 79, 116, 161–162, 167–169
hair sculpture, 116
hair shafts. *See also* hair follicles
  defects in, 83
  formation of, 5–8, 18–23, 82, 157
  growth pattern of, 16–25
  keratins in, 82–84, 92
  melanin in, 94–97
  pigment in, 94–97
  structure of, 4, 80–82
  types of, 18
hair shampoos, 91
hair shape, 89–90
hair stylists, 79, 88, 116, 161–162
hair transplantation, 163–166
hairstyles, 56–60, 65–66, 90–91
Halfdansson, Harald, 55–56
Hamilton, James, 45
Harris, Richard, 101
hat-making, 86–88, 124–125
hatters, 86, 125
healthy body, 46–47, 63
healthy hair, 46–47, 63–64, 81–83, 105
heat transfer, 9–13
Hendrix, Jimi, 56–57
Henry III, King, 137

INDEX